"Would You Ever Teach Us to Read, Sister?"

by

Sr Colette Dwyer SHCJ
her Colleagues
and Travellers

BLACKWATER PRESS

Editor
Deirdre Bowden

Design & Layout
Tony Dunne

Cover
Philip Ryan

© Sr Colette Dwyer 1995

ISBN 0 86121 667 9

Produced in Ireland by
Blackwater Press
c/o Folens Publishers,
8 Broomhill Business Park,
Tallaght, Dublin 24.

All rights reserved. No part of this publication may be reproduced, stored in a retrieval system, or transmitted in any form or by any means, electronic, mechanical, photocopying, recording, or otherwise, without the prior written permission of the publisher.
This book is sold subject to the conditions that it shall not, by way of trade or otherwise, be lent, re-sold, hired out or otherwise circulated without the Publishers' prior consent in any form of binding or cover other than that in which it is published and without a similar condition including this condition being imposed on the subsequent purchaser.

Printed in Ireland at the press of the Publisher.

Contents

	The Travellers' Friend	iv
	Foreword	v
	Dedication	ix
1	Childhood and Early Life	1
2	Religious Life and Teacher Training	7
3	Work in England	11
4	Return to Ireland	15
5	The Travellers — A Chance Encounter	21
6	Early Work	25
7	Into The West	31
8	Progress in Educational Provision	37
9	Attempts to Meet the Demands for Employment	43
10	Who are the Travelling People?	47
11	Some Friends and Colleagues	57
12	Contributions from Colleagues	69
13	Travellers' Views on their Educational Experience	91
14	Dreams and Hopes for the Future	97

The Travellers' Friend

Have we thanked thee Colette
for the love you have given,
and for helping the Travellers
in their way of living?
and have we not told you
we hear and we see
what you are doing
for Travellers like me?

We know of the nights
that you lay awake
thinking and planning
for the Travellers' sake,
and this I can promise
when e'er it should end —
we'll remember Colette as
The Travellers' Friend.

Gus Sweeney
(Traveller)

Foreword

I HAVE chosen this title for the book, which recounts the development of education/training and employment for Travellers over a period of 28 years, for two reasons: the first that it was spoken to me by a Traveller woman five days after my return to Ireland after an absence of 32 years (at a time when we were never allowed home), and the second that it was the sentence which brought me into the final phase of my life and work, which has turned into the most productive, and for me fulfilling, period of all.

I have not written the book myself — something which I have often been urged to do — the vast majority of it has, in fact, been written by Sr Cyprian Unsworth, who has lived with me, worked with me and tolerated me for over twenty years. Without her I could not have accomplished half of what I have been able to do at my age, with my many disabilities and limited talents. Herself an invalid now, and bedridden for the last six years after suffering a massive coronary, the strong will which impelled her to undertake this work has enabled her to see it through. In one of the two chapters which I have written myself entitled 'Some Friends and Colleagues', I talk about Sr Cyprian more fully.

As is recounted in this book, I was always drawn to working with the most needy in society. While teaching during the war in a secondary modern school (for the least able pupils in English society) my experiences led me to tell the English Provincial Superior that I felt my vocation lay with such children — a view which was subsequently ignored. I had already received an earlier rebuff when I told my Novice Mistress that I felt called to work in our African Mission. She looked down at me from her great height (she was very tall) and said scornfully, 'You, Sister? You would not be worth your fare out'. However, the desire remained, and was at last more than fulfilled once I had met the Travellers. Now I feel that the work of the last 28 years has been the most important of my life, and probably the main reason why God made me and put me into this world.

I was going to include President Mary Robinson in Chapter 11, but realised that the best must be kept for the beginning. She has been a tremendous inspiration to me since the day I first met her in Wicklow Circuit Court, where, with her great attraction towards the marginalised and most needy members of our society, she was giving of her very special skills as a barrister to defend Traveller families when they were being victimised and unfairly treated. In the last case in Wicklow she defended nine very poor families against Wicklow County Council and a very 'anti' group of settled families in whose housing estate they had taken up residence. When the Judge gave his verdict against the Travellers and in favour of the residents the President took their case to the High Court, and when she failed there, to Strasbourg. The nine families involved in that case are now happily settled in the accommodation of their choice, near enough to St Kieran's School for them all to have been able to attend it.

I was indeed proud to be asked to take part in her campaign for election to the Presidency, and no one was happier than I when she was duly elected. She has proved to be such a wonderful ambassador for Ireland all over the world yet has never lost her special love for the least respected in society. I was very privileged to be able to

Foreword

arrange the first visit by Travellers to Áras an Uachtaráin, where she treated them with great warmth and understanding. They came away holding their heads very high indeed. I am proud to have had the opportunity to know her, and to know at firsthand the esteem in which she is held by the Travelling people.

Despite the Presidential example there has, sadly, been a great deterioration in the attitude of the settled community to Travellers in some parts of the country over the last 12 months. As this book is really about educational development, it does not address such key issues as discrimination, accommodation and marginalisation. One must not ignore the level of hatred, manifesting itself in ugly, almost Nazi-type, violence against some Traveller families, a hatred which clearly has profound repercussions on every aspect of Travellers' lives. To confront these attitudes the Government must, I feel, take very firm action.

Sr Colette Dwyer SHCJ
September 1995

To Sr Cyprian SHCJ, without whom this book would never have been written, nor many of the events described in it been able to come to fruition.

1

CHILDHOOD AND EARLY LIFE

COLETTE Dwyer (christened Therese, and always called Rosemary until she became a nun) was born on 17 April 1917 in Arbutus Lodge (now the Arbutus Lodge Hotel) Cork. Her earliest memories were of a happy, carefree childhood spent in this lovely house, with its gardens sloping down to the River Lee. She was the third child of her father, Walter Dwyer, a self-made but very successful business man, of Dwyer and Co., Washington St, Cork, and his third wife, Marie Goldie. Rosemary found herself with a ready-made family of already adult brothers and sisters, some of them married and with young children. The best known of these was probably Willie Dwyer, who founded Sunbeam Wolsey, and several other subsidiary companies, as well as building the fine Church in Blackpool for his workers and their families known to this day as 'Billy Dwyer's fire-escape'! Indeed he needed no fire-escape, as he was a man of boundless heart and kindness.

One of Rosemary's earliest memories was of the arrival of the Black and Tans in Cork, which caused her mother and father to move from their beautiful home in Arbutus to a house in St Anne's, Blarney. Her happy childhood continued there, and she has vivid memories of, for instance, being held upside-down by the feet to kiss the Blarney Stone. She also remembers making her First Communion 'in disgrace' at the age of seven — she was so uncontrollable that her parents took her to see the Bishop, who advised them to allow her to make her First Communion! On the morning of the appointed day, she was found by her 'Nanny' licking the condensation drops on the glass of the front door, and was thereby deemed to have 'broken her fast', so her Communion had to be postponed to the following day. Her parents had actually asked the Bishop to exorcise her, he refused but she has no recollection of the effect his recommended alternative had on her behaviour! However, the happiness of her childhood years continued in St Anne's with her older sister Maureen, brother Dermot and the youngest and most angelic of the family, Colette.

Following the sudden death of her father (who was nearly 40 years older than her mother) in 1928, Rosemary was sent to school in England along with her two sisters, where she encountered the Holy Child Sisters for the first time at St Leonards-on-Sea in Sussex. She was a delicate child, and her mother knowing nothing of English schools, had chosen St Leonards from a telephone directory, reasoning that it would be a healthy place as it was by the sea. On such strange coincidences depend much more significant events, as it was to the Order of the Holy Child Sisters that Rosemary turned years later when the conviction that God wanted her to 'be a nun' could no longer be avoided!

While still at school, her mother remarried, and Rosemary, her brother and sister found themselves with a step-father, who was Russian, whom she grew to hate and fear. He had clearly married her mother for money and not love, of either her or her children. While courting he had made great play of loving the children and years later Rosemary's mother confided that she had married him because 'you children needed a father, and he seemed so fond of you'. He treated her mother very badly, and cruelly, while making very unwelcome advances to Rosemary and disliking Maureen and Dermot. He was a drunkard to boot, as her mother discovered on her wedding night. Nevertheless, she stuck with him through eighteen years of cruelty, violence and shame, in spite of urgings from her Confessor, her doctor and all her children to leave. She always answered such requests with the words 'I took him for better or worse' and was faithful to him, in spite of his many infidelities, until her health finally broke down, and she was forced to leave him.

Rosemary's eldest sister, Maureen, ran away from home during the period following the marriage, and years later Dermot confided in Rosemary his belief that 'our childhood ended the day she married again'. On reflection the only blessing arising from this unhappy time was that Rosemary developed very early in life a great understanding of children who were unhappy or abused at home. This stood her in good stead in the years ahead when she was teaching and caring for children and young people. They often used to say to her 'you are so understanding, I never thought I could talk about these things with anyone'. It also made her pray that she would be worthy of her mother. The family lived in London while the children were at boarding school, but returned home to Ireland for the summer.

On passing her A-levels and leaving school, Rosemary spent a glorious year in Rome, where the Holy Child Sisters had their Mother House. Here they took students from all over the world, ostensibly to learn Italian. Rosemary did learn Italian, but soon tired of 'more lessons', and made life very difficult for her unfortunate teachers. There was so much to do and see in Rome! Mussolini was at the height of his popularity and one of Rosemary's favourite ploys was to go with a few friends to the Piazza Venetia, and stand outside the window of his rooms chanting: 'Duce!, Duce!', until he would appear when the Piazza was full to address the adoring crowds. Rosemary felt it gave her great 'crowd control'.

Nevertheless, while she enjoyed the life of Rome to the full, she also became very interested in the spiritual and religious aspects of the city. Her immediate response to the first inkling that the religious life might be her ultimate destiny, was a determination to resist at all costs. While in Rome she decided that she wanted to make a career on the stage, and even made an application to a drama school as a sort of 'escape policy'. She also proceeded to be as 'difficult' a student as possible so that the nuns would not have her! She succeeded very well in this plan, as the Head of the Order told her years later on the eve of her reception into the Novitiate that she had had the unique experience of telling the nuns at St Leonards that Rosemary had applied for reception, and been greeted with almost universal horror, voiced by one of the nuns in the words 'Don't take her Reverend Mother. She will wreck the Order!'

When her half brothers in Ireland, who were her trustees, heard of her love/hate relationship with the notion of religious vocation, they suggested that she go on a 'world tour' to dissuade her from such an unsuitable idea. Strangely enough, this suggestion had the opposite effect to that intended, and shortly afterwards she promised Our Lady, during Mass in the little Church of Our Lady of Good Counsel that for better or worse, she would give it a try. When she wrote to the General of the Order to ask whether they would have her, she told her of her brothers' suggested alternative, the reply said: 'That is wonderful, because you now have the chance literally to choose the Lord instead of the whole world'.

Childhood and Early Life

Rosemary responded to her decision by resolving to enjoy life to the full during her remaining months of freedom, thus causing the nuns in Rome many a headache! On one occasion she remembers being locked out of the house late one night, and having to throw pebbles at the window of one of her favourite nuns who let her into the 'enclosure' to smuggle her back. Rosemary was instructed to 'close her eyes and see nothing'!

On another occasion, irritated by being constantly reminded by the nun in charge to take a tonic prescribed by the doctor, she took the whole bottle in one go. Unfortunately it contained arsenic and had a very strange effect on her! She was amused by the ensuing fuss, not aware that the nuns had phoned the local chemist, who instructed them to send for a doctor without delay! By the time the doctor arrived, resplendent in evening dress from a smart party from which he had been summoned, she had walked into a door splitting open her eyelid, and been violently sick — the latter probably saving her from a worse fate! The nuns had already prepared a table by her bed with the necessaries for the Last Sacraments and sent for the priest!

When Rosemary told her mother she was going to be a nun, she took it very well, as was in her character. Rosemary did not really fully realise what it must have meant to her, as she was the last of her children to go — leaving her alone with her tyrant husband. Many years later, when she was old and ill, and Colette (as she then was) told her she would leave the Order to look after her, her mother was adamant — she had given her daughter to God long ago and would never take back that gift.

2

RELIGIOUS LIFE AND TEACHER TRAINING

IN September 1935 Rosemary entered the Novitiate at the Order's Provincial House in Mayfield, Sussex. She found, as most people did, the six months as a postulant followed by the two years as a novice very difficult in every way, petty and restrictive, and apparently leading nowhere. Of the ten who entered with her, only four survived to make Final Vows. Though she often contemplated leaving, something (or Someone) always held on to her, and she was professed two days after her 21st birthday, taking the name of Colette, her youngest sister, who had died tragically at the age of 11 from meningitis, following an epidemic of measles. Her death had been a great blow to her mother, and Rosemary felt that taking her sister's name might console her a little.

Colette had begun having fainting fits during the last few months of her Novitiate and her Superiors had become increasingly worried about the state of her health. She was sent to the small convent in Fribourg which took students from different countries. The convent was situated between the Alps and the Jura mountains and Colette spent six very happy months there rejoicing in the beautiful scenery. The Superior, a Frenchwoman, had a great love of mountain-climbing and would hire a guide to help little parties of nuns climb the more difficult peaks. After only six months of this unique experience Colette was recalled very suddenly to England, and to her old school at St Leonards, where an unexpected vacancy had arisen on the school staff. She taught French, which she spoke fluently, and the nuns, many of whom remembered her from her own school days, teased that she would now understand what she had put them through! It did not turn out like that — Colette found that although she lacked formal training she had a natural aptitude for teaching, and ability to relate to young people. She soon built up a reputation for being 'strict but fair' with her students, and was quite sad when the outbreak of the Second World War interrupted this first experience of the classroom.

When war broke out it was soon recognised that Sussex was one of the counties most at risk from German bombers and Colette was sent with two elderly nuns to Torquay, where it was decided that a suitable place should be found to which the school could be evacuated. A building was finally procured and the evacuation of the school, with all its attendant furnishings, began. Unfortunately, an adjacent property, a former hotel, was later commandeered by the Royal Air Force as a convalescent home for wounded airmen, and from that time the area became a target for enemy raids. On one occasion Colette remembers sitting on a bench commanding a beautiful view of the sea with her Superior when a fighter plane swooped down and proceeded to spray the area with machine-gun fire. The Superior, with great presence of mind, dived with Colette underneath the bench, and the plane continued to the RAF home — its intended target.

Shortly after this incident the school and community were evacuated once more, this time to Coughton Court a haven well inland under no threat of attack, owned by Lady Throng-Morton, who lived in one wing of the house. The children loved the surrounding countryside, and especially the arrival of the newborn lambs in the adjoining fields!

In 1940 Colette was sent to study English language and literature at St Anne's College, Oxford. Four years of great happiness and fulfilment ensued under an exceptionally liberal and gifted Superior, Mother Marie Therese, who became one of her greatest friends and most formative influences on her life. She always said how fortunate she was to be at Oxford during the war years, as, with most of the male students away at war, the female students enjoyed for the first time the riches of having tutors such as C. S. Lewis, Tolkien, David Cecil etc.

Although still attired in the long black habit and veil, her Superior insisted that Colette must participate as fully as possible in all the activities of the students' lives, and this she gladly did. She never found herself ostracised in any way by her fellow students, who included her in everything. During those war years, all the students were expected to give so many hours a week to 'war work' of various kinds. Colette chose to work in Lord Nuffield's munitions factory where she tested bullets. About 20 workers sat around a long table, and each one had to apply a different test to each bullet. If the bullet was unblemished, it was placed in the 'out tray' to the left. In the meantime, the 'in tray' to the right was filled by an adjacent worker applying a different test. The accumulation of bullets in the 'in tray' was therefore an indication, immediately apparent to all, that you were not keeping up. This work gave Colette some insight into the stress engendered by having to do a repetitive job at maximum speed for hours on end.

During her first year at Oxford, it was compulsory for all the students and members of the Community to repair to the air raid shelter in the garden every evening at 6 o'clock, and there continue as best they could their routine of study and prayer, until the 'All Clear' sounded. Fortunately Lord Nuffield, a very successful business man and benefactor of the city, had provided a fleet of 100 fighter planes which circled the city every night thwarting German raids. Oxford was never bombed.

Shortly before her final examinations, Colette was admitted urgently to hospital with acute appendicitis. She was still in bed, though at home, when the examinations began. Fortunately, her Superior was allowed to invigilate, supervising her for six hours every day of the examinations, and making sure that all was done according to the rules. Despite these difficult circumstances Colette got the desired results.

On leaving Oxford, she had to complete a year of supervised teacher training in University College London, but the College had been evacuated to Blackpool, where the Order had a large school and community, so she went there. Here again, the war favoured her, because so many of the male teachers had gone to the front she was allowed to teach practically throughout her year of training. She was sent to a secondary modern school (in those days the secondary moderns were for the less gifted children, who had not 'made it' to the other secondary schools) and was given the 'E' stream to teach. She felt completely at home with these least able children, most of whom came from very disadvantaged homes. At the end of her year's training, she told the Head of the Order, 'I think my vocation lies with children like these' to which the Provincial Superior replied, 'I will bear that in mind, Sister'. Colette spent the rest of her 32 years in England in the Order's schools for the most privileged children! However, she always said that she loved all children, whether they came from very wealthy homes or, as in the later years, the poorest and most disadvantaged.

3

WORK IN ENGLAND

In 1945, Colette, her studies completed, was posted to Combe Bank, a large boarding school in Kent, built around a magnificent house which had belonged to a very wealthy family and surrounded by beautiful grounds. The nuns lived in the basement, while the rest of the main house and its many extensions comprised the school.

Colette was appointed Form Mistress, teaching english, history and religion to various higher classes, although she was herself still in her twenties, and only a few years older than her oldest pupils. To the children though, all nuns were 'old', and she well remembers a child asking her at the end of a lesson on costume through the centuries, whether she had worn a crinoline before she became a nun! She never had any problems with the children, but much too soon in her eyes, as she loved teaching, she was made Headmistress, and remained in that position until she left Combe Bank in the early 1950s, when she was appointed Headmistress of Mayfield, the Order's Mother House, a much bigger school located in a picturesque Sussex village. Colette found herself with some hundreds of students, and a staff which soon rose to 50 or more. It was here that she met up again with Sr Cyprian Unsworth who had been in the Novitiate with her. She was a very popular member of Colette's staff, affectionately known to her students as 'Cippy', and now known to her myriad of friends by the same name! However, when she was moved from Mayfield to the north of England, their paths did not cross again for nearly 20 years.

One of the first things that struck Colette when she became Headmistress of Mayfield (which had just amalgamated with St Leonards, her old school) was that the numbers were so large that a form of institutional living would prevail. She therefore decided that the school should be divided into 'houses', of about 50 students of a cross-section of age groups, and each with its own House Mistress and House Captain (one of the sixth form). In a comparatively short time, with the blessing of the 'powers that be', houses were built, and a system implemented which remains to this day. Inter-house competitions in sport, drama, music, etc. developed over the years, and there was a healthy rivalry between houses. The school was very fortunate in having a fully qualified, and exceptionally brilliant architect on the staff, Sr Nesta. With great ingenuity, because of the restricted nature of the campus, she designed all the new buildings which gradually mushroomed around the main school house. The students experienced their first swimming-pool (an outdoor one, but later a magnificent indoor heated one was built).

Colette enjoyed her years at Mayfield — always happy when there were plenty of children around, and finding that these particular children, although far more richly endowed with material goods than the ones she had worked with hitherto, had their own very real needs, coming, as many of them did, from broken homes or, more frequently, from families where one or more parent was absent, sometimes for long periods of time. In spite of the fact that to such children Mayfield was indeed 'home', and very close relationships developed between them and their favourite nuns and teachers, Colette remained implacably opposed to boarding schools as such, feeling that all children needed to grow up in the family environment.

4

RETURN TO IRELAND

In 1967 Colette was sent to Ireland, after an absence from her native land of 32 years, during which time (according to the strict rules of the day) she was not allowed to visit her home and family, though they could visit her, and frequently did.

She was appointed Superior of the Holy Child Convent at Killiney in Dublin where there was, and still is, a large and flourishing school. Colette decided that she should leave the running of it completely to the Headmistress, as she herself had suffered, as had many others in the same position, from Superiors who tried to run the school through the Headmistress. This meant that for the first time in her religious life she found herself without children, and she missed them enormously. However, within a week of her return, she had found the children with whom she would spend the next 28 years of her life — the children of the Travelling Community.

In the meantime, one of the major interventions of God in the direction of Colette's life which occurred at regular intervals throughout it, took place.

She had felt within a few days of her return to Ireland that Holy Child nuns were not engaged in Ireland in the work which the Order's foundress, Cornelia Connelly, had set out to do, i.e. to teach to 'all classes of children'. The school in Killiney was doing excellent work, as was the hostel for working girls in Dublin, but the underprivileged were not being educated anywhere in the country. She had said this to the Provincial Superior within a few days of her return, and told her that she also had been invited to visit the Archbishop of Dublin, the redoubtable John Charles McQuaid, at his request, very shortly. Colette asked her Superior if she could suggest to him that the Order would be interested in starting a free secondary school in the Archdiocese. It was 1967 and free post-primary education for all had just been introduced by Donagh O'Malley, the dynamic Minister for Education. The Provincial warned her to be 'cautious', but gave the idea the go-ahead. Wanting to be fully prepared for any questions the Archbishop might put to her, she had followed up her request by looking around for a suitable location. On her way from the airport the previous week, she had noticed the name 'Sallynoggin' on a bus she had passed and was immediately intrigued by it, so when one of the older nuns asked her if she would like to go for a walk on the following Saturday, she said she would like to visit Sallynoggin. It was about an hour's walk from Killiney, and when they arrived there they were confronted with vast housing estates teeming that afternoon with children of all ages, and almost as many dogs! There was a huge church at the end of the road, and walking up to it Colette met a woman and asked her where the local schools were. The woman pointed out a prefab building beside the church, and when Colette asked her about secondary schools, she replied, 'Well, there's Joseph of Cluny up on the hill there, but you have to pay fees to go there, so most of ours end at primary'. Colette entered the church, and said to the Lord, 'If this is where you would like us to be, please help me'.

A few days later Colette met the Archbishop and put

forward her proposal, he asked her where she was thinking of, and when she answered 'Sallynoggin', his incredulous delight was blatant. 'You mean to tell me that the Holy Child nuns would go to Sallynoggin', he said. Colette replied that that was what she hoped, and only discovered later that it was one of the poorest and most crime-ridden of the new areas springing up everywhere on the outskirts of Dublin. The Archbishop said he had Church land between the primary school and the church, which the Order could purchase for £10,000!

The next step was a visit to the Minister for Education, Donagh O'Malley — a wonderful character. He told her he had never heard of Sallynoggin, got out a huge map of Dublin and its environs, and asked Colette to point it out to him. He asked Colette whether she had consulted with the Secretary to the Department, Sean O'Connor (later to become one of Colette's greatest friends and supporters), she said she had but that he did not seem very keen on the idea. The Minister immediately phoned him in Waterford. When Sean came on the phone, the Minister said to him, 'I have an interesting lady called Mother Colette with me, and I think she would like to have a word with you' and promptly handed Colette the phone. She told him it was about the school in Sallynoggin, and he replied, 'Yes, it's completely out of the question that Holy Child Sisters should go there' — he probably had the idea that Holy Child Sisters only taught in schools like Killiney! Colette must have made some reply to the effect that she was disappointed, because the Minister lent across his desk saying 'I'm the Minister, not him', Colette hastily handed him back the phone. After a brief exchange, the Minister hung up and told Colette to go ahead with the purchase of the site. She had no problems with the Department after that. Sadly, Mr O'Malley, widely acknowledged as the best Minister of Education ever, died very suddenly three weeks later.

It was decided that the school would be comprehensive in nature and would cater for 800 children — it became the first community school in the country. Colette held that as school was a place where children went to learn how to learn, not just to learn 'facts', she wanted the school built around, and leading into, an unusually large library. One of the things which had shocked her on her return to Ireland, was the absence, or inadequacy, of libraries in so many of the schools she visited. She also wanted the school to embody her idea of cross-fertilising of age groups throughout the school, so it was to be built in four houses, each to hold 200 children in an assembly area on the ground floor, and all four houses leading into the library. These large social areas could each be sub-divided into four classrooms, and the entire building was to resemble the shape of a St Brigid's cross. Colette was very fortunate in her architect, Edward Brady, who took into account in his plans her vision of what she wanted the school to embody.

Another aspect of Irish education which had struck Colette on her return was that all the school principals she met were either nuns or priests or brothers. She made it known from the beginning that all posts in the new school would be open to all teachers, whether they were were lay or religious, male or female. So the first principal and vice-principal, when the school opened its doors in 1970 were lay people. The Order had also made it clear to Colette that, due to the diminishing number of teachers in the Order, not more than two sisters would be allowed to have posts in Sallynoggin. One of these was for many years the Head of the Religious Education Department, and the other was the School Secretary. The latter quickly established herself (unconsciously) as the centre of the school and, together with the Head of Religious Education, succeeded in making it a 'real Holy Child School'. Colette remained on as manager, and soon built a strong management committee of gifted people with various kinds of expertise. When the Lord made it clear to Colette that she was to follow a new 'calling', she knew the school was well established and built on strong foundations. And so its future development has shown.

5

THE TRAVELLERS — A CHANCE ENCOUNTER

WHILE the development of Sallynoggin Community School was in progress, the work with Ireland's Traveller Community, which was to become the main work of Colette's life, had already begun.

Once again, the Lord pointed the way, and showed her very clearly which direction she should take. Within a week of her return to Ireland in 1967, she was walking down the road outside the convent in Killiney, when she came to a field in which nine Traveller families had set up a temporary camp. Appalled to find that during her years away, so little progress seemed to have been made in the lot of the Traveller Community, she went into the field and was immediately surrounded by a group of men and women, and about 40 children. As a child Colette had believed the lives of Travellers to be romantic and free but she was now confronted with the reality of the many hardships they had to endure — no water, sanitation, or other amenities of modern living. A few of the families in the field had barrel-top wagons, the rest just the traps which they used for shelter when not travelling. She felt helpless in the face of so much human misery, and wanted to do something to alleviate it, so

"Would You Ever Teach Us to Read, Sister?"

before leaving them she asked 'Is there anything I can do to help you?'. To her surprise one of the women said, 'Would you ever teach us to read, Sister?,' Colette replied, 'Well, I've been a teacher all my life, and if you'd like, you could come up to the convent at the top of the road this evening, and we'll see what we can do'.

To her great astonishment, that evening over 30 men and women came to the convent, and followed Colette down the main staircase to the children's dinning room. A few of the Sisters had offered to come and help her out. When the Travellers were all seated at the tables, Colette looked around thinking, 'It's true that I'm a teacher, but I've never had a class quite like this before'. Wanting to give them an immediate experience of success, as any good teacher would, she asked 'What word would you like to learn first?' One of the men replied, 'Sister, you know those yokes at the end of roads that tell you what to do when you're driving your vans around? Would you tell us what they say?,' and she realised that though most of them drove vans, none of them could read the road signs — let alone the directions written on them. A shiver ran down her spine, as she realised that they didn't know what S.T.O.P. meant. So they began with that. Then she turned to the women, and said, 'You don't drive vans, do you?' (they do now, of course) and asked them what words they would like to learn first. One of them replied very shyly, 'You know when we go to the shops to get the messages, we never know whether we're buying flour, or sugar, or what's in them packets, and we do be ashamed to ask the girl to tell us'. This reply made a profound impression on Colette, and she often said in later years that, more than anything else it was what made her decide that if this was God's Will for her, she would spend the last years of her life working for the education of the Travelling People.

The Travellers — A Chance Encounter

'God,' she said, 'Help me to be allowed to do this, if it is Your Will'.

The adult classes grew and grew, and nuns, priests, students, etc. joined Colette to teach the Travellers on a one-to-one basis to read and write. Some months later, the parents began to bring their teenage sons and daughters to class with them. Teacher numbers swelled to about 40 to cater for the increased demand to learn. However, when children, some as young as six were brought Colette realised that they could not possibly learn at night classes — what was needed was a school.

As the school at Killiney was fully occupied by its students during the day she set about looking for suitable premises elsewhere. She first approached the local parish priest in Ballybrack — as she had noticed an empty school building in the grounds of the church there. Although he personally was very sympathetic, he said that a parish committee had charge of the old school and its uses, and he would have to ask them at their next meeting to consider the request.

This he did, and subsequently rang Colette to tell her they had said they couldn't possibly let 'itinerants' into the school, as it was used once a month for ICA meetings. (Later, members of the ICA called on Colette, and told her they had not been consulted, and certainly would not have been against it.) Some time later, when Colette had still not been able to find anything suitable in the area, members of the parish committee called on her, and said she could use the building in the mornings, as long as the toilets and water were not used, and that no chairs or tables were brought into the building! They also mentioned that the Protestant Church on Killiney Hill had an empty building in its grounds, which she could possibly get permission to use. To this she replied that she would be ashamed to have to tell the Travellers that their own Church had refused to accommodate their children!

After many fruitless efforts, the school, with 15 pupils and one teacher, was finally established in two rooms generously offered by a Quaker lady, Ms Sheila Pim, in Old Connaught Avenue, Bray. She was a member of the newly-formed Committee for Travellers, which had recently come into being following a brilliant lecture given in Bray by Victor Bewley and Fr Tom Fehily — the real pioneers of the movement. This Committee, which Colette had also joined, later became the National Council for Travelling People and was joined by some 80 committees from every county of Ireland. Twenty-five years later it lives on in the National Federation of Travelling People and one or two other smaller groups. The greatest change within this movement is that now more and more Travellers play integral parts and are increasingly taking a leading role in setting the agenda by expressing their own hopes and aspirations for their community.

6

EARLY WORK

THUS came into being the first special school for Traveller children — St Kieran's School, still going strong today, 25 years later, and with over a hundred children in attendance divided between six classes and a pre-school. After several weeks in Old Connaught Avenue numbers rose to almost forty and the Marianist Brothers in Loughlinstown offered Colette the use of two prefab classrooms. In 1969 an old Christian Brothers School together with seven acres of land was bought for £25,000. Five homeless families moved into the now-redundant five prefab classrooms on the site, which had been converted into small houses. Three of those families have since been housed — the other two have remained. When the word got around that the Travellers' Committee had bought this land, there were the kind of protests and pickets which we still witness to this day. The Traveller families eventually had to be moved onto the site in their caravans in the middle of the night, with a garda escort. All the usual myths about 'devaluation of property' were promulgated, but as it turned out, there has never been any trouble with our neighbours, and the land immediately opposite the property was bought by a developer, sold for thousands of pounds, and bought by people who wanted to build luxury houses at astronomical prices!

During the next ten years the school had to move three or four times. The 'red brick school' had been burnt to the ground in 1974 (caused by an electrical short-circuit in the attic of the one hundred-year-old building), and in 1986 the prefab building which had replaced the burnt-out school finally, and literally, collapsed. A bigger and more permanent school thus became a necessity. Colette discussed it with the parents, who were absolutely horrified at the thought of St Kieran's going out of existence and was faced with the fact that, as they put it, they had learned everything they needed to know there, leaving it self-confident and proud of their Traveller identity, and they wanted the same for their children, and their children's children! She felt that, since they were allowed so few choices in their own destiny, they should not be denied this point. The necessity for a new school became a reality in 1990 with the opening of the new St Kieran's Primary and Pre-School.

When the 'red brick school' was opened, the Archbishop of Dublin, John Charles McQuaid, had told Colette that he would like to come and bless it, as he was then nearing retirement. He duly did so, and several years later his successor, Archbishop Dermot Ryan, likewise came to the opening of the next school, which preceded the school's final resting place in the new building. When he visited the families on the site, one of the little boys living there rushed up to him, seized his hand, and covered his ring with kisses. Archbishop Ryan looked down at him from his great height and asked, 'Who taught you to do that?' The boy peered up at him and said, with a jerk of his thumb 'Sister Colette when the other fella came'! The 'other fella', John Charles, would have been highly amused at the description!

While she was still living in Sallynoggin, and establishing St Kieran's Colette began travelling around the country

Early Work

conducting the first survey of Traveller children nation wide, with particular emphasis on their educational needs. The picture it revealed was bleak — less than 150 children attending school regularly out of a possible 10,000.

When this first survey was concluded she sent copies to the President, the Taoiseach, the Minister for Education, and to the Press. As a result, she was invited by Jim Sherwin, who at the time did a weekly interview programme on RTE called 'The Church in Action', to appear on the show the following Sunday. She agreed readily, and it was only when she saw the television studio, cameras and other equipment that she realised that she was actually going to give an interview which could be heard and seen by other people. For the first, and last, time in a studio, she became panic-stricken. Jim noticed that she had gone deathly white and asked her whether she felt alright, to which she replied, 'Actually, Jim, I think I'm going to faint'. Jim was horrified, and asked whether he could get her anything to make her feel better as they were going on air in about two minutes time — she replied that the only thing which might help her would be if he was really interested in what she was going to say. He assured her that he was indeed very interested, and that was why he had asked her to come on the programme.

In the event, that was exactly what happened. Jim showed his genuine interest in what she had to say about the Travellers, so she was able to talk quite naturally about her experiences as she had journeyed around the country, getting to know Traveller families in every county.

As it turned out, this interview marked an important turning point in the whole story of her future work with the Travellers. In the course of the interview Jim asked her what sort of reception her report had received from the Minister for Education. Without pausing for thought she replied,'A had immediately expressed her desire to relocate with Colette, so together they spread out a large map of Ireland on the floor of the kitchen, and finally decided that Clare would be the most central county from which to do their work, since it was adjacent to Galway, Limerick, Kerry etc. They set off on the mission to find somewhere to live in their Renault 4, and spent a week looking at a number of very unsuitable possibilities. On the final day Colette said to the Lord at the beginning of Mass, 'If you want us to come and live in Clare please send us a message in the Readings'. The first one began 'I will have vengeance, says the Lord,' which was not very helpful, but the Responsorial Psalm, Psalm 23, contained the lines 'I will lead you by quiet waters to rest your drooping spirit'. Colette took no message. Leaving the Church they met a friend they had made in Feakle, who asked them how the house-hunting was going, when they said they had found nothing, she said, 'Have you seen Fr Harry Bohan's bungalows on the edge of Lough Graney?'. They said they had not, so she turned the car and five minutes later they were in Flagmount, where six bungalows looked over the beautiful lake, Lough Graney. Four of them were already sold, but one, the second along, was empty. Looking out over the still waters of the lake, Colette heard again the words of the Psalm, and they knew that they had found where they were meant to be.

They called the house 'Quiet Waters'. It cost £5000 and made a perfect home for them for the next 13 years. The bungalow had a small entrance hall, which they turned into an oratory, a large living-room, a small kitchen, two small bedrooms, and a larger one which became a visitors' room, occupied for two-thirds of the year by many guests. There was a small grassy patch in front of the house, and at the back a good-sized garden, where Colette grew vegetables and fruit. Tomatoes and strawberries were also cultivated in a little greenhouse built by a kind neighbour, Rodger Moroney.

The European Provincial Superior, Sr Anne Laing-Brooks, came to see the bungalow one cold blustery April day before the decision to buy was made, 'Well, it wouldn't be my cup of tea,' she said, 'but if you and Sr Cyprian think it would be a suitable place from which to do your apostolic work, we had better take it'. At Easter 1976 they moved into the little home which the Lord had found for them.

Flagmount village consisted of a church, a school, a shop which doubled as a post office, and a scattering of houses — no pub! The latter fact provided Colette with one of her first local 'good works' — ferrying old men the few miles to the nearest pub at night (but never bringing them back, as fortunately, it was understood that someone else would give them a lift home — a most necessary act of charity!) The people of Flagmount gave them a great welcome when they arrived, anxiously enquiring when were they going to build their 'proper convent' never having dreamt of nuns living in a bungalow! When they first heard the nature of the Sisters' work, they were sceptical but soon got used to the fact that there was to be no 'big convent' and no Traveller families living in the haggart!

Although the Sisters were not able to do much work in the village itself, owing to the nature of their apostolate, they did succeed in organising a choir. This was much appreciated by the congregation, and further strengthened by the acquisition of a small organ, which enabled them to extend the range of their repertoire. Later on, a drama club was set up, which produced the first plays ever seen in the village. Sr Cyprian made wonderful costumes, and the plays of Synge, Yeats, as well as an annual Nativity Play, attracted large and appreciative audiences. When Colette heard that most of the children had never been to Dublin, or indeed anywhere by train, she arranged to take them to see Maureen Potter in her annual pantomime. They were enchanted by the whole experience, beginning with seeing railway carriages with notices on the windows stating 'Reserved for Sr Colette's Flagmount party', which they carried off on the return journey as mementoes. When Maureen Potter actually named the 'Flagmount Drama Club' among her list of people attending the performance, they nearly fell over the edge of the balcony with incredulous delight. Now, of course, there is an excellent post-primary school in Scariff, eight miles from Flagmount, with drama as a subject, and the Scariff Players have achieved nationwide fame.

Some 12 years later the Sisters had to make the sad decision to leave Flagmount owing to a deterioration in Sr Cyprian's health, and to move somewhere where there would be better access to public transport, doctors, hospitals, etc. The people were almost as sad to see them go as they themselves were to leave Flagmount — the most beautiful village overlooking Lough Graney, the Lake of the Sun, over which they could see the sun rise and set each day.

As before, a long spell of house-hunting in the Ballinasloe/Galway area, eventually led them to a housing estate, on the outskirts of Oranmore — within easy reach not only of Galway, but also a very large population of Travellers, and, above all, immediate access to the main roads east to Dublin, south to Cork and Limerick, and north to Sligo and Donegal. This made Colette's travels so much easier.

The bungalow they got permission from the Order to purchase was in a 67-bungalow estate, which they had turned into one evening on their way home after another day of fruitless searching. It was exactly what they were looking for, even though there was no lake, no visitors' room, and no view, except of the long rows of similar bungalows in front of and behind them. They missed the more intimate life of the village, but they quickly made new friends with a number of their neighbours — most of them retired couples or young families with small children. Galway is alive — full of music and art, and festivals celebrating the rich culture of the Gaeltacht and Connamara. The latter had become their most beloved spot even while they lived in Clare, and they had always tried to take visitors to see it — now it was 'on their doorstep'!

Only a little more than a year after their move to Galway, Sr Cyprian suffered a massive coronary, from which she was actually declared dead by the local GP and also on admission to hospital. Colette stayed outside the Intensive Care Unit all that night, and the next day begging the Lord not to take her, unless she was going to be severely mentally or physically damaged. The doctors did succeed in reviving her but lost her twice again that day, the first time for 35 minutes. The medical team fighting for her life, under the leadership of Dr Kieran Daly, did not give Colette much hope, and eventually had to operate, without anaesthetic, to insert a pace-maker. They showed Sr Cyprian what they were going to put in, telling her it was the latest model from Germany, with a ten-year guarantee. She asked how much it cost, and when they replied that it was probably the most expensive thing she had ever been 'next or nigh to' (it was £25,000) and that she had better get Sr Colette to take out a life insurance on her, she told them to put away their knives as she was an Old Age Pensioner, and couldn't possibly afford to pay for it. 'It's all free, Sister,' said Dr Daly, 'no wonder Ireland's such a poor country,' she retorted immediately and the operation went ahead.

After a long sojourn in the Intensive Care Unit,

"Would You Ever Teach Us to Read, Sister?"

Sr Cyprian was moved to a small ward adjoining the nurses' room. One afternoon, when Colette was not with her, she awoke to find an enormous flower arrangement on the bed-table which she had pulled up to her neck to give her some privacy from the many people who were visiting their relatives in the afternoon. She exclaimed aloud 'Well, if they think I'm dead, they've got another thing coming'! and went back to sleep. Later she heard that the beautiful flowers were a gift from St Kieran's School, and had been delivered while she was asleep!

After many weeks in hospital, she was finally allowed to come home, but the doctors told Colette that she would probably only live for a few weeks, as the wall of her heart had been so badly damaged by the violence of the coronary. That was six years ago!

8

PROGRESS IN EDUCATIONAL PROVISION

Having completed the work in the area of primary education, Colette realised that there were a number of crying needs in the whole programme which needed to be addressed.

During the early 1970s Colette founded the *Association of Teachers of Travelling People* (ATTP) as the ever-increasing numbers of teachers involved as Resource Teachers had very little contact with one another, and she felt there was a growing need for a forum at which to meet and share their experiences. The association held regular meetings, and is still in existence today — some 20 years later.

Soon Colette also realised the need for pre-school education, as the Traveller children, no matter how intelligent they were, always seemed to be at a disadvantage in mainstream classes, either because of the fact that their home background was inevitably disadvantaged — no books and little hope of support from their parents with their school-work — or because, in the early days, the majority of them came to school at a later age, and often missed school because the family was travelling. In fact, it soon became clear that the growing desire among adult Travellers for 'a fixed abode' on a site or in houses, was largely inspired by their great desire to send their children to school 'to become scholars', as they put it. Tribute should be paid to the many and great sacrifices made by thousands of Travellers to ensure this basic human right for their children.

When Colette first approached the Department of Education for pre-schools for Travellers, to give them a 'head-start' when they reached an age for entry to mainstream education, she was told that the Department had never, and probably would never, pay for pre-school education. The intervention of a Minister and a number of supportive officials soon dispelled this view, and when Colette retired as National Co-ordinator there were 53 Traveller pre-schools in existence. A number of them are now staffed by Travellers who have themselves been through the educational system, and taken further qualifying exams. In pre-school, the children learn a large number of skills — hand-eye co-ordination, basic reading and writing, socialising skills, educational play etc. By the time they are old enough for junior infants they are now much more able to hold their own than ever before.

While a number of children went on to secondary education in many parts of the country, Colette quickly noted two trends: (1) they were learning very little, and (2) few were staying on long enough even to be able to qualify for what was then called the Intermediate Certificate, now the Junior Certificate. Most of them gave up within weeks of entering secondary and/or vocational school. Often they had to contend with the open opposition of their parents, who felt that they should have learned all they needed to know at the end of their primary years. In the Traveller Community, children are held to be adult at the age of 12 — Confirmation is regarded as graduation to adult life, and thereafter, their services are often required at home, either to mind younger siblings or help with scrap and horses etc. Naturally this appeals to the majority of them far more than a return to school routine.

In 1978 Colette started the first Junior Training Centre, for the 12–15 age-group. The first Centre was located initially in Booterstown, in premises loaned by the Mercy Convent, and then moved to Milltown Park, in the grounds of the Jesuit property there. After a while the idea caught on, and other similar centres began springing up in different parts of the country. The centres' programme was divided between 'academic work', i.e. reading and writing — for the many who either never went to primary school, or left without basic literacy, practical work — to which the children are very attracted, using their very considerable skills in working with wood, art, gardening, building etc., and sport, for which again they have a great love. It is clearly apparent that children in this age-group come to school for two reasons only — they like their teachers, and they like the programme on offer. If they do not, the incentive to attend quickly evaporates, and, as always, there is rarely any pressure from home on them to attend.

The VECs finance the Junior Training Centres, but of course the children attending them are not paid (that would be illegal), therefore the decision to attend has to be made by each child. Of course, the first priority is to encourage them to go on to the local post-primary school, but only a very small percentage of children in this age-group avail of that choice, and 12–15 year-olds remain the biggest challenge facing all those involved in Traveller education.

The appointment of Visiting Teachers was one answer to that challenge. Acting as liaison officers between schools and families they proved a godsend to the harassed Colette, who was trying to service the needs of the whole country, driving up to 1000 miles a week, most weeks. These teachers encourage parents to make the often considerable efforts to educate their children. The first Visiting Teacher was appointed in Galway, and her success in reducing the number of children not attending school to 12 within a very short span of time, and in helping the children with their homework in the evenings on the camp-sites, with the assistance of young voluntary teachers, made the Department more amenable to appointing more Visiting Teachers as time went on.

The first Training Centre for Travellers, St Kieran's, catering for 15–25 year-olds was established in 1974 in the burnt-out remains of the old red brick building. There are now 26 of them across the country, financed by FÁS and the VECs, with around 600 trainees, male and female, attending them.

The trainees follow a programme which takes account of their literacy needs, introduces them to computers, gives them social life skills, and offers personal development courses, as well as a large selection of practical skills — metal-work, copper-work, carpentry, cookery, crafts of all kinds, hairdressing etc. The general aim of the programme is to prepare the trainee for life and, hopefully, for employment. Unfortunately, the 48 weeks allowed to each trainee to complete the course, are inadequate to cover the educational gaps in the majority of trainees' lives. At the minimum a two-year course is needed, when one realises that for many the course has to compensate for the 12 years of education which the majority of the population has received before they are able to apply for an apprenticeship or further training. The end result of this situation is that what could be an excellent opportunity for members of the Traveller

Community to 'catch up' with their peers in the settled community, is being stifled at birth. Appeals for a two-year course have always been countered by the claim that Europe allows a maximum training period of only 48 weeks for European Social funded training courses. Many more young Travellers would be equipped for the labour market if a more realistic approach were adopted.

9

ATTEMPTS TO MEET THE DEMANDS FOR EMPLOYMENT

IN the early 1980s Colette discussed with a group of friends consisting of Michael Bermingham, Director of St Kieran's Training Centre, John Tansey, a long-time supporter of the education/training and employment of Travellers, Padraig White, Director of the IDA and others, whether there was anything which could be done to provide preferential employment for Travellers. They all agreed that the need was urgent in this area, and that an Enterprise Centre should be established — the first thing that needed to be done was to find a site.

Colette approached Barry Desmond, the Chairman of Dublin County Council, always known for his concern for the under-privileged and marginalised. He agreed to make an acre of land available on the new Sandyford Industrial Estate. A little while later, Colette received a bill from the County Council for £10,000, which she promptly forwarded to Barry Desmond, saying she thought it must have been sent in error, as she understood that the land was a gift! She never heard anymore about it.

An excellent architect was identified by John Tansey, Jack O'Keefe, Principal of Bolton St College of Technology, and he speedily drew up plans for a perfect industrial complex on the site provided. It consisted of a two-storey administration block, and nine small workshops. The latter were to be leased out to potential employers, who would sign contracts agreeing to employ half their workforce from the Traveller Community. In exchange they would pay reduced rents, and have the use of other facilities such as the fax, photocopying machine, and boardroom in the main office. A centre manager would have overall responsibility for the choice of potential employers, collection of rents and the administration of finance. In addition a personnel officer would not only identify suitable potential employees, but also oversee the way in which they were treated, what wages they were paid, and generally look after their interests. Before their work could begin and the workshops filled, however, the buildings had to be completed, and much funding found. Colette and her friends set about this task with a will. The Youth Employment Agency, under the leadership of Niall Green, was then in existence and supplied generous loans (later turned into a grant), and the Bank of Ireland, whose Governor at the time was Bill Finlay, was also very amenable to helping out with a substantial loan — most of the repayment was subsequently waived.

The money was finally raised, and St Kieran's Enterprise Centre, the first serious attempt to provide employment for Travellers, was officially opened by Garret Fitzgerald, then Taoiseach of the Coalition Government, in 1983.

One of the very encouraging developments of the last number of years, is the increasing number of young Travellers who are going on to third level education or further training. Some have obtained university degrees, others have qualified as teachers, others again as community workers. So the dream has come true of Travellers being able to provide their own community with the services for which

Attempts To Meet The Demands For Employment

hitherto they were dependent on members of the settled community. This could probably be described as the ultimate goal towards which the whole structure of educational opportunity is geared.

10

WHO ARE THE TRAVELLING PEOPLE?

THEY are a minority community of Irish people, part of and living in the main community of Irish people. That is how they see themselves. If you ask Travellers almost anywhere in Ireland how they see themselves in Irish society, they will invariably answer 'We're Irish people,' or sometimes 'We're Irish Travellers,' despite the fact that many of them are settled in houses for many years — some of them even for their whole lives. Unfortunately, the question of their identity has been somewhat muddied during the last decade by well-meaning people who felt that it would be more advantageous to them (from the point of view of EU grants) to be given an ethnic identity. This is something which the majority of Travellers all over the country strenuously reject, as they see it as in some way detracting from their full membership of the Irish race, and even, in some cases, as being one more label which is affixed to them, along with 'itinerants', 'knackers' and other less acceptable terms.

There are over 3000 families of Travellers in Ireland at the last count, and over 2000 of them have chosen to settle either in houses, on properly serviced sites or in group housing schemes which can accommodate an extended family. This leaves over 1000 families on the side of the road, living in appalling conditions without any modern amenities. It is true that many Travellers, not surprisingly, have retained the 'nomadic' characteristics of their forebears, and love to 'take to the roads' in the spring and summer. It is also true that many young couples, when they get married, choose to move into a trailer during the early years of their married lives, even though so many of them were born and reared in houses.

One of the main factors motivating so many families to 'settle' has undoubtedly been the ever-increasing demand for education for their children. Colette has always said that in her work of promoting educational opportunities for Travellers, she has been very aware of the danger that education might, in some way, deprive them of their unique and precious heritage. Nevertheless, as previous chapters have outlined, educational programmes have been instigated as a response to Travellers' own expressed desire to learn. The title of this book surely reflects this.

The prejudices harboured by members of the settled community against this small minority in our society are difficult to comprehend, and can only be explained by the profound ignorance from which they spring. Often Colette, when speaking to various groups of people who have expressed a wish to know more about Travellers, begins by asking how many people in the audience have ever spoken to a Traveller, or visited a Traveller site. It is rare if more than one or two have. On the whole, Travellers are judged by the settled community by what they see on the side of the road.

To dispel the myths one by one: Travellers are, by choice and inclination, probably the cleanest members of our society. Colette first discovered this 28 years ago, at the night classes in Killiney. Opposite the room in which the classes were held was a small cloakroom comprising a toilet and handbasin. Into this Colette had put soap and towels, and she told the group on the second night of their classes that it was there for their use whenever they so wished. It was quite extraordinary to see the response. Men and women (always one sex at a time) crowded into it every evening, and washed as much of themselves as they could reach without actually undressing. They would come into class with clean hair, and shining faces, never ceasing to wonder at the miracle of hot and cold water at the turn of a tap.

One of the first families Colette got to know, and whose friendship she enjoys to this day, lived in a muddy field in a trailer — mother, father and ten children. Their mother washed all their clothes by hand in often icy cold water, brought back to the camp in large milk churns from a source eight miles away. Yet the children, like their home, were always spotlessly clean.

Travellers make incredible efforts to keep themselves and their camps/sites/houses clean against all the odds. Colette remembers an occasion when a group of seven families were unofficially parked, the ground around them littered with what their more fortunate neighbours would have put in their bins. She asked the Travellers whether they would like a bin for each caravan, and when they said they would love it, she and her committee provided each family with one. At the end of the week the Corporation was asked to collect and empty them but Colette was told that only householders could have rubbish collected, so the bins overflowed. When we lived in Clare we actually had no refuse collection or indeed water, apart from the village well, but we were fortunate first of all in not having ten or twelve children, and secondly in having convents in Dublin which we visited most weeks taking our sacks of rubbish, and our plastic containers for water with us. What struck us most was the amount of rubbish which we accumulated and could not dispose of, just the two of us, each week.

Many people object, not unnaturally, to Travellers who beg on the streets. Experience has taught that unless the family circumstances are known money should not be given, and food or clothes only when there is a real need. Very often the majority of Travellers who come to the door are not looking for hand-outs, but more often for friendliness and even a chat over a cup of tea. Travelling women often have their own special friends among the settled community, and they resent other Travellers encroaching on their own particular 'ladies'.

Once Colette saw two little boys begging on the side of the pavement in O'Connell Street, Dublin. As she approached she saw that the younger one was crying — his tears falling like a waterfall onto the ground in front of him. As Colette approached, she saw the older boy give the weeper a vicious pinch, saying 'Cry harder, you'. Colette stopped in front of them (she knew the family), and began severely 'If I ever see you pinching Mick like that again...' At this point a well-dressed women passed by and threw a 50p piece into the boys' collecting box. 'I wish you would not do that,' Colette said immediately at which point the woman looked at her with some disdain saying, 'It's all very well for you, Sister, with your warm Convent and three good meals a day, but I just wanted to make sure that these two little boys can get something hot to eat on this bitterly cold day (it was February). I wonder how much time you ever spend thinking about these children'. 'Quite a lot of time, as a matter of fact,' responded Colette continuing, 'If you think these children are going to be able to spend any of the money they are given on buying food for themselves, you have another thing coming. Johnny and Mick will go back to their caravans to-night, and hand over their 'takings' to their father, who will probably go off and spend it on drink. He will come back some time during the night and, if the drink has made him violent, will probably beat up his wife, and possibly his children too, and so, because it has proved lucrative, the practice of putting children out to beg, especially in the cold weather, will continue.' While Colette was speaking, Johnny (the pincher) took the 50p out of the box, and flung it back at the lady, as much as to say, 'Listen to her. She is telling you the truth'.

Drunkenness is often associated with members of the Travelling Community, however many surveys carried out by the Gardai and others on drunkenness among Travellers have shown that the problem is no more widespread, some would say even less so, than sample groups of the settled community. Whereas the latter generally drink either in the privacy of their own homes, or, more often, in pubs, Travellers, while publicans are happy to sell them alcohol, are rarely permitted to drink it on the premises. So, in many cases, they are compelled to drink by the side of the road, or in some other public place. Hence the well-known stereotype of the 'drunken Traveller'. Another factor which must be taken into account is that Travellers often eat very erratically, and everyone knows that drinking on an empty stomach is a recipe for speedy intoxication. Quite apart from Travellers, all poor people, when they are cold and hungry, tend to become intoxicated by smaller amounts of alcohol.

Travellers are perceived as being 'very wealthy' people. Few Travellers have bank accounts, instead they choose to invest all they have in a van or car — essential for transporting their large families, the reality is that what you see by the side of the road represents the entire 'wealth' of the family. Few of them have jobs, or any chance of getting them, although many of the younger ones, having gone to Training Centres, or even in some cases to third-level education, are more than qualified. The trouble is that few employers want to give them a chance once they know that they are members of the Traveller Community. The extravagance of their weddings is also often criticised. One cannot presume to dictate on such matters. Travellers have great skills as traders and some are very sucessful in business and are indeed quite rich. In Co. Limerick some wealthy Travellers have built magnificent homes for their families. These they inhabit for about six months of the year, spending the period from March to August on the road selling their wares.

Well-intentioned advice and intervention by the settled community can have very serious consequences on the lives of Travellers.

Colette learned very early on in her work with Travellers of the dangers of suggesting any kind of family planning. An inexperienced social worker had persuaded a young mother of nine, whose children were attending St Kieran's School, to take 'the pill'. The consequences were immediate and disastrous. The young women told a friend on the site that she had been given a pill to take which would stop the babies 'coming so fast'. Her husband heard about it, and within days three terrible things happened. First, he beat her to within an inch of her life. Second, as the news of what she had done spread, she was named 'Mary the Pill' on the site, and, third, and perhaps most serious of all, her children became known in the school and elsewhere as 'Ellen the Pill', 'Mick the Pill', 'Ned the Pill', 'Mag the Pill' etc. Shortly afterwards they left the school, and the family moved to another county.

Another example of the harm well-meaning members of the settled community can inadvertently cause, was when a little boy who was short-sighted and having difficulty with his reading, was taken by a well-disposed member of the local Travellers' committee, without any consultation with his parents, to the local hospital to have his eyes tested. Glasses were recommended, and in due course he was given a pair. The day after he went home to the site with them, he and all his brothers and sisters were taken away from their school. Colette immediately visited the field in which the family were camped, and met a very angry mother, who said she would never allow her children to go to school again. Colette tried to explain, while apologising that the action had been taken without the parents' consent, that the child was now able to see the letters in his school-book more clearly, so he would learn to read more quickly. She asked the mother why she was so opposed to glasses. 'God gave us the eyes he meant us to have', was the reply 'and we shouldn't be trying to change them'. It was, in fact, only then that Colette realised that she had never seen a Traveller, adult or child, wearing glasses.

Much has been said about the many criticisms levelled against Travellers, but how do those who have lived and worked among them for decades, regard them? Colette has always said that their good qualities far outweigh the objections voiced by many. She has always found Travellers to be loyal, generous to a fault, with a deep and strong religious faith, and is proud to count many of them, old and young, among her closest circle of friends.

Travellers never withhold their trust and friendship once it has been given, and can be relied upon always to give their support in times of need. They are intensely dedicated to their families, and almost aggressively defensive of them. They look after their own until death. It is also interesting to note the strong bonds which exist between the older and younger members of a family, however large. Recently when the first ever Traveller to be elected to public office was chosen, by settled people as well as Travellers, to represent their interests as a Town Commissioner, and later chosen for a 'Person of the Year Award', it was a matter for surprised disbelief on the part of society in general. On the other hand, those who work with Travellers wonder only why it has taken so long for people to recognise their worth. Travellers should be regarded as full members of Irish society, with the same rights and entitlements as every other member of society. Their strong and rich culture should distinguish, and not isolate, them from Irish life.

We feel for them in the isolation which so many want to impose on them, and admire the way in which they have succeeded against all the odds, and in increasing numbers, to reach out to third-level education. It is indeed rewarding to see them now being able to take over work hitherto the preserve of settled people, among their own people, so that gradually we become redundant in these areas.

So we come back to our original question 'Who are the Travelling People?' This has inevitably involved dealing with some, though by no means all, of the many pre-conceptions about them which seem to be so widely held by members of the settled community. Naturally the Travellers are deeply hurt by the hostile attitudes they encounter so frequently in the course of their daily lives. They long to be accepted for who and what they are, and treated like everybody else, unless of course they have personally, by unsocial behaviour, forfeited such a right. To know that communities in towns

Maureen (left) and Rosemary with their mother, 1918.

Walter Dwyer, Colette's father.

The last photograph of Rosemary before she entered the Novitiate in 1935.

Colette with Mayfield children.

Archbishop John Charles McQuaid with Colette and the first staff of St Kieran's School, 1972.

Michael Birmingham, Gene Fitzgerald (Minister for Labour), Colette and John Tansey at the official opening of St Kieran's Training Centre, 1975.

Sr Cyprian and Colette visiting a Travellers' site in Dublin.

Sr Cyprian and Colette celebrating their Golden Jubilee in 1988.

The new St Kieran's Primary and Pre-school.

President Mary Robinson presents Colette with a 1991 Pensioner of the Year Award.

and villages across Ireland say openly that they do not want them living in or near them — tarring all Travellers 'with the same brush', and blaming all for the crimes or transgressions of the few, is deeply resented, especially by the younger members of the Traveller Community. The very fact that their sites are so often located on rubbish dumps, or well hidden from the eyes of the rest of the local community, sends Travellers the very clear message that they are shunned and rejected by society at large.

11

SOME FRIENDS AND COLLEAGUES

I HAVE chosen to write this chapter myself, as no one else can really know all the people — lay and religious, women and men, Travellers and settled people — who have helped and advised, encouraged and inspired me down through the years in my work to achieve basic human rights for the Travelling People of Ireland.

Right at the top of the list must come Sr Cyprian (Cippy, as we all call her) who has lived and worked with me for over 20 years. An Englishwoman from Lancashire, she possesses all the best qualities of the nation and county from which she comes, allied to a strong and deep love of Ireland and the Irish. We were, as she has related earlier in this book, thrown together very much by circumstances, and have lived together in a community of two for over 20 years.

At the age of 81, and after the massive coronary described earlier, she undertook to write this book, as she felt it was a story that should be told, and one which I had refused on many occasions to contemplate writing myself.

She is loved and revered by many members of the Traveller Community who visit her even to this day, and never fail to enquire about her when I meet them without her, or when they write or telephone me.

She has been a wonderful companion to me, so much so

that I cannot imagine life without her. She has championed me when things have been bad, advised me when I did not know where to turn, consoled me when black clouds seemed to surround me, and on many occasions encouraged me to keep trying, although in latter years she has worried that I am still doing far too much, and would often try to persuade me to say 'no' to invitations to go thither and yon, to 'put up my feet' sometimes and give in to the growing tiredness. Her sense of humour has been constantly in evidence, and her sharp wit and intelligence have remained, fortunately unimpaired even by the severity of the coronary which actually caused her death, and present precarious health. As a 'patient' whom I have the privilege of nursing, she never makes any demands, never complains, or even asks for anything, but constantly thinks of others, and does not want to cause anyone 'trouble'. During her early years with me, I benefited by having one of the widely recognised 'best cooks in the Order' living with me. Now, her efforts have been seriously curtailed, as she is on a regime of almost total bed-rest. As my skills in the culinary area are very minimal, she has to be satisfied with ready-prepared dishes and the microwave yet she never grumbles.

Without her patient but persistent work and pressurising, this book would never have been written.

As mentioned earlier, my first contacts in my work with Travellers were Victor Bewley and Father Tom Fehily. Victor was an inspiring leader of what later became known as the National Council for Travelling People, an organisation entirely geared towards meeting the needs of Travellers. He enjoyed the total confidence of successive Government Ministers, and was for many years adviser to the Minister for the Environment. His own strong faith and total commitment to the policies of the Society of Friends were a constant source of inspiration to the members of the National Council.

When Victor asked me to take on the role of National Co-ordinator for the Education of Travellers, I had monthly meetings with him in his small office over Bewley's in Westmoreland Street as Victor was at the time still Manager of Bewley's. I found these meetings, which always included lunch, very inspiring, as he would listen to my reports on the previous month's work, and then bring his great wisdom and understanding of the Travellers to bear on particular problems which had arisen. This was an invaluable apprenticeship for someone working in an area so different from anything which I had experienced before in my life of teaching and administration, and for which there were no precedents.

Father Tom, now Parish Priest of Dun Laoghaire in Co. Dublin, was another great stand-by person, who helped me in innumerable different ways. Together with Lady Wicklow and Victor, Fr Tom was a founder member of the National Council. He was also a member of the First Commission on Itineracy set up by Charles Haughey in the 1960s under the leadership of Judge Brian Walsh. Fr Tom has never lost his interest in the Travellers, and quite recently made generous efforts to help me to sort out some of my most pressing financial problems.

Not long after I was asked to take over the responsibility for Travellers' education, I met Joyce Sholdice, who had been appointed as the first National Co-ordinator for Accommodation a few years before me. We worked very closely together, and in the early years, even travelled together. She introduced me to contacts she had already made while working on her own and we also exchanged notes on our findings. In any particular town or county,

Joyce would visit County Managers etc., while I went to schools and educational officials. We would generally stay in small (inexpensive!) hotels frequented by commercial travellers, and would meet in the evenings, after completing our rough notes, and discuss the day's events over an evening meal. However, as I grew into my work, our paths diverged more, though we always remained in close contact with one another, and eventually ended up living in the same estate in Oranmore! Joyce later succeeded Victor Bewley as Chairperson of the National Council.

Sadly, tensions which later developed in the Council, put Joyce's work under intense pressure, and her doctors advised her to cut all her ties with the Travellers' work for health reasons. Eventually the National Council was dissolved, on a motion put forward by a young Traveller man, and was replaced by two separate organisations — The Federation of Irish Travellers (FIT) and the Irish Travellers' Movement (ITM).

Another great friend of the Travellers was the late John Charles McQuaid, Archbishop of Dublin. He lived beside our convent in Killiney, and frequently summoned me to meetings concerning Sallynoggin, and the growing work with Travellers. When the 1968 Chapter of the Order, which was held in the United States and attended by me, decreed that we should change our long black habits into something more suitable for the various works in which we are engaged, I returned from it to Ireland (and Killiney) attired in a short blue skirt and overblouse, with a short blue veil, which had been given to me in the States. The Archbishop sent for me, presumably to 'inspect me'. I duly presented myself and his first words were, 'So this is the new Holy Child habit — well, well...' I said, 'you don't like it, Your Grace?,' he replied, 'It's not that I don't like it, but I would pass you in the street, and

I would not know who you were'. Needless to say the chances of 'passing me in the street' were minimal, as he was driven daily from his Killiney home to the Diocesan Headquarters in Drumcondra! A short time later, the then Provincial Superior of the European Province came to Killiney on a visit, and asked me to accompany her to pay a courtesy call on the Archbishop. I remained in his chapel while they met. Later she told me that when she went into his study he examined her from head to foot, and then remarked, 'I am very glad to see that you are properly clothed, Mother, not like that lady in blue downstairs'.

On another occasion, I was told there was a call for me on the phone from the Archbishop's House, thinking it was our Chaplain, and the Archbishop's secretary, who had been on holidays, I said, 'Hello Father. Is that yourself?' To which the well-known voice replied, 'No, Mother. It's the man next door'.

When John Charles died, he was succeeded by Dermot Ryan, who became a great friend of mine — much to the surprise of many of my friends. Shortly after his consecration as Archbishop, he paid an official visit to Sallynoggin Community School. At the time I had a number of problems which were weighing heavily on me, but as manager of the school, I was busily seeing that everyone had something to eat and drink after the ceremonies. Suddenly I was aware of Dermot Ryan's tall figure standing beside me and he said quietly, 'Are you worried about anything Reverend Mother?' I was so taken aback that I replied, 'Not really Your Grace'. He went on to say 'If you ever feel it would be a help to discuss anything with me, don't hesitate to let me know'. I felt that God was saying something to me through this totally unexpected invitation, and soon afterwards I contacted Dermot Ryan, and a regular series of meetings took place between us, initially in Drumcondra, and subsequently at his own home in Ballsbridge. He proved to be a very wise counsellor, and I was devastated by his early removal to Rome, and subsequently his sudden early death.

Another great friend and supporter in the Church with a long record of service in the Traveller Community was Des Williams, the Auxiliary Bishop of Dublin. He later became Patron of the Federation of Travellers which succeeded the National Council.

During my 25 years as National Co-ordinator for the Education/Training of Travellers, I have worked with nine different Ministers for Education — some good, some hopeless as far as the needs of Travellers were concerned.

Far and away the most committed to the cause of education for Travellers was Mary O'Rourke. This was all the more unexpected in that the relationship which developed between us began on a very inauspicious note. Very shortly after her appointment as Minister she had to implement swingeing cuts in the education budget. She had hardly begun to learn her new brief when she had to face the Teachers' Meetings in Easter Week. While speaking to the TUI she told them that they need not worry about the cuts as far as their VEC schools were concerned, as these could be applied to such 'peripheral issues' as prisoners and Travellers. Her speech was relayed on radio and TV, and naturally I was furious. RTE rang me that night and asked for my reaction, which I duly gave.

In the meantime, the Minister was interviewed on *News at One*, and when asked how the teachers had taken her announcements about the cuts, replied that they seemed happy enough. The interviewer said he knew of one person who was anything but happy, Sr Colette Dwyer, the National Co-ordinator for Travellers' Education. She replied that she would be seeing me on the following Saturday, and she was sure I would be happy after our meeting. RTE rang me again and asked me to go on the Sunday News Programme after our meeting, and I readily agreed. Mary asked me to come to her home on the following Saturday, and when I arrived said that she had been very badly briefed by her Department about Travellers' education needs, and asked me to fill her in on the whole area. Two hours later, when we had covered the entire issue, she asked me what I wanted her to do first and when I replied, 'Promise me that while you are Minister no cuts will ever be allowed to interfere with our educational and training programmes'. She gladly acquiesced, and that day began a wonderful era of co-operation between us. When RTE asked me on the Sunday News Programme how our meeting had gone, I was able to say that I had been completely satisfied with the Minister's commitment. They asked whether I thought she would really honour it, to which I replied, 'If she doesn't, you will be the first to know.' Mary O'Rourke and I had many meetings often at her home in Athlone, as new problems arose, and I always found her as good as her word.

The person most closely associated with St Kieran's, and still there to this day, is Rose Lamb. She has been co-ordinator of all the out-of-school needs, provided the children's daily meal, supervised non-academic staff, caretakers, school bus drivers etc. She is patient, though fair, with all, and much loved by the children and their parents. In fact, it is difficult to think of the school without her. When we moved into the new school, she immediately took on the responsibility for the care of the surrounding grounds — beautiful flowers were growing around it almost before we moved in. She is also Secretary to the Board of Management, and takes many burdens off my shoulders by her devoted service to all the school's needs. I personally could not have gone on as manager all these years without her.

When the Training Centre began, in the burnt-out shell of the old school in 1974, its first Director was Michael Bermingham, the newly-retired Principal of a local VEC school. During his years in the Training Centre, he set in motion all kinds of imaginative programmes and projects, and, in the early years, before a financial package had been put in place whereby AnCO (as it then was) and the VEC each paid a portion of the overall costs, he thought out and applied his incredible energies to raising money for the centre, such as an 'Annual Day for St Kieran's' in the local golf club. He also inaugurated the annual Display and Sale of the trainees' work at the Horse Show and Spring Show, which was manned for many years by Cippy and me, ably assisted by such gifted people as Mena Darcy (now the longest-serving teacher in the Centre), Joan Merrigan, with her many artistic skills, Kathleen Kinsella, keeper of the accounts and retired Secretary to the Board of Management, and many more. Mena Darcy still does wonderful work with the girls in the Centre, producing patchwork of an incredible standard. She has taught cookery, dress-making, and other handicrafts to generations of young Traveller women.

Tribute must also be paid to the teachers, beginning with the first teachers in the adult night classes, who gave so generously of their time and expertise. Anne Dempsey became the first Vice-Chairperson of the ATTP (Association of Teachers of the Travelling People) to which she rendered invaluable service. In our own Order, Sr Audrey was the first Sister to take up a full-time post in St Kieran's School, and later Sr Sheila joined as a teacher in the adult classes. Then, of course, came Sr Cyprian, whose pupils in the adult classes still remember her with affection, and always ask after her.

In the wider field of my work on a national level, I have been much helped by the ever-increasing number of local committees, most of which had originally been affiliated to the National Council, and have now transferred their allegiance to the National Federation of Irish Travelling People. Like the Council, the majority of these committees give their services on a voluntary basis, but increasingly are being joined by social workers, and others active in delivering services to the Traveller Community. The Federation also enjoys the full support and expertise of many other people — teachers, local authority officials, officials of the Department of Education etc. Loretta McVeigh is currently co-Chairperson, with traveller Paddy Ryan, of the organisation. She has been involved in every aspect of Traveller need — accommodation, education, training and discrimination, for over 20 years in Carlow Town and County. She was the moving spirit in setting up the very successful Carlow Training Centre, which she helped to become an Enterprise Centre by developing both a furniture business and some of the most highly-acclaimed copper-work in the country.

Another great woman, who is a household name in the world of Traveller craft, is Sr Brigid Keane, who, ran the first Girls' Training Centre in Galway City, and later developed a thriving shop in Galway's Fair Green, which is now run by Travellers as a Co-op. The shop has won the franchise for making the President's flags, and also exports flags and banners world-wide, even to the United States.

Father Shaun Curran SJ was the first Administrator of the first Junior Training Centre in Booterstown, for 12 – 15 year olds, staffed by a combination of Primary and VEC teachers. His leadership, and total affinity with young Travellers was one of the main reasons for its success. Young

Travellers between the ages of 12 and 15 are recognised to be the most difficult of all to integrate into a school atmosphere, but in the special environment created by Fr Shaun and his staff, the two sole prerequisites for their attendance — love of their teachers, and a programme which caught and held their interest — were in place. Fr Shaun would begin his day by driving one of the two school buses for many miles, as the catchment area for the new school was very wide, collecting the majority of the pupils from halting sites and delivering them to school.

Although he is no longer involved in the actual running of the centre, following heart by-pass surgery, he still plays a key role in its development, under its new and dynamic Principal, and the numbers have risen to between 20 and 30, which is rare for any centre catering for these children. Love has been, and continues to be, the key-note, and the active programme of improving literacy skills, plenty of practical work, and a generous allocation of time for sporting activities have ensured that it will continue to grow and flourish.

The whole world of Training Centres and Junior Training Centres opened up new opportunities for friendship and links with new Travellers and their families, as well as teachers and other colleagues. This is the place where I can pay tribute to them all. I will finish with Paddy Houlahan, a friend and colleague whom I first knew as Director of the first Training Centre in Ennis, Co. Clare. Now living in Galway, he has remained a wonderful friend for the last 25 years both to Sr Cyprian and to myself. He has such a 'way' with the Travellers, that he is almost one of them, and his songs about them and their life-style have won him personal acclaim. The Furey Brothers have included his 'Living on the Edge of the Town' in a recent album.

I must thank television and radio producers in RTE, and

the Press, beginning with Jim Sherwin, referred to earlier, Gay Byrne, Stephen Collins, Anne Dempsey, and many, many others, who provided the right kind of publicity when it was most needed. For example, in the very early days John O'Donoghue's publicising of the fire in St Kieran's School resulted in money pouring in to rebuild it. Later others followed such as John Bowman and Marian Finnucane. The contribution made by all of these was essential in changing public attitudes towards Travellers and their problems.

Finally, I must pay tribute to John Tansey, who is almost as much a part of my work as I am myself. He has been with me since the beginning — the first committee, the first classes, the first school, on whose Board of Management he still sits, the first Training Centre, on whose Board of Management he still sits, the first Employment Centre, on whose committee he still sits — to all of these projects he contributes his great store of wisdom and expertise. To me he has been available for wise advice whenever I needed it. In fact I don't think I could have done without him. Thank you, John.

If I began to name the Travellers who are my friends and colleagues this would be a very long chapter indeed — but they are among my closest circle of friends — a circle which blessed the final years of my life.

12

CONTRIBUTIONS FROM COLLEAGUES

This chapter contains personal reflections on the life and work of Colette from some of her friends and colleagues.

MY FIRST contact with Sr Colette was at a meeting about Travelling people in Dublin in early 1980. Soon after she took the chair at that meeting. I realised that here was no ordinary nun. She had a magnetic presence and was totally committed and single-minded in the pursuit of the interests of the Travellers. Wafflers, and those tending to overelaboration were quickly brought to book with a look or a pithy phrase.

In time, I began to realise that this steely aspect of her character was tempered by a very humane and compassionate nature. I also became deeply appreciative of her determination and stamina during the many battles that lay ahead in pursuit of the goal of providing Training Centres for teenage Travellers. Thankfully, she was a formidable adversary as well as advocate in her determination to facilitate Travellers in achieving both their potential and their rights in society.

In the early days of the Training Centres especially, her ability to negotiate and to be taken seriously at the highest level were essential in getting the question of Traveller education onto the agenda of the statutory bodies. More importantly, she was instrumental in having issues dealt with the urgency which they demanded.

I was fortunate to experience her negotiating skills at first hand on one occasion. She was dealing with the 'top brass' from FÁS and the Youth Employment Agency, and she invited myself and another director along for 'moral support'. As it turned out our role was akin to the 'spear carriers' of Roman times. Apart from a few perfunctory remarks on our part, she more than capably stated our case. My abiding memory is of the manner in which she put the various officials at ease, assumed control of the meeting, and by a combination of charm, guile and sheer negotiation ability, succeeded in achieving her objectives. Characteristically, after the meeting she stressed the importance of our support, and suggested that she couldn't have managed without us!

Obviously her commitment and dedication impressed people at every level. This was vital at this juncture, as the setting up of the Training Centres required an innovative approach, and a level of risk-taking and commitment by members of the statutory agencies. If all else failed she would not fail to make a direct appeal to the humanity and conscience of the officials concerned. Given her own lack of vested interest, this could be a devastating weapon. It was very hard to say 'No' to Sr Colette, and I can say that from personal experience. I still cannot visualise any other single person who would have been able to galvanise decision makers, and produce the co-operation between them necessary to ensure that the Training Centres got off the ground. In relation to the setting up of St Finbar's, one of 27 Training Centres in different parts of the country, she certainly showed that her persuasiveness, and transparent selfless commitment, were difficult for many a local official to counter.

She was also the catalyst which unified and produced action from the various strands of activity happening at local level. In relation to the setting up of St Finbar's Training Centre at its present location, she was always willing, at short notice, to drive to Cork and act as advocate, especially as it related to dealings with Cork VEC, FÁS or Cork Corporation. While we each had our own areas of experience and expertise, she had a vast reservoir of information and arguments at her fingertips, and was able to quote chapter and verse as to the situation in various other parts of the country.

In pursuit of her goal, she followed a punishing schedule, in support of the various Traveller Committees around the country. This routinely involved clocking up to 1000 miles per week traversing the roads of Ireland, sometimes at a breathtaking pace. On one occasion I recall she wrote off her car, but this was brushed aside as a minor irritation, a blip on the onward march of progress.

She, along with Sr Cyprian, frequently visited us in Cork, and she had a special affinity with the place because of her birth and upbringing there. She was greeted by a mixture of awe and respect by the trainees, as her reputation had preceded her. I was always struck by her facility to recall the names of trainees she had met on a previous visit, and to unravel intricate family relationships.

She always insisted that we must listen to the views of Travellers, and let them tell us what they want, rather than trying to impose our opinions or philosophy on them. This approach was clearly signalled in her Annual Report in the early 1980s and those which followed it.

In relation to participation in schools, she advocated 'integration without absorption', and she was always alert to the dangers of subjecting Travellers to the influence of an

"Would You Ever Teach Us to Read, Sister?"

Such unswerving determination, I always thought, must come from a deeply felt motivation. One senses a firmly-held Christian faith underlying her work, but without overt display. Her personal lifestyle has always been simple, unostentatious — austere even.

I feel that her work for the betterment of Travellers is based on more than a sense of duty to 'do good'. I believe that her real personal interest and concern shows clearly in her encyclopaedic knowledge of individual Travelling families, a knowledge which she carries lightly, but which always amazes me.

Sr Colette is a doer; a pragmatist rather than a polemicist, getting down to doing things of practical benefit rather than haranguing the public about the rights of minorities and "ethnic groups". She has been the prime mover in bringing about Traveller education and training in Ireland.

John Tansey

I FIRST met Sr Colette when I went to work in the office in St Kieran's Training Centre in Bray in 1977. My husband had died a year previously and I decided that I must look for a part-time job to supplement my widow's pension as I still had three children at school.

My job was to assist Michael Bermingham, director of the Centre, but I little thought what started as a part-time job would become one of the most enriching experiences of my life. There I met many people who unselfishly gave of their time and commitment to improving the lot of the Travelling People. Central to all of this was Sr Colette — how can one describe this truly remarkable woman?

Long before anyone else gave 'a damn' she saw the need

Long before anyone else gave 'a damn' she saw the need and, indeed the great yearning, for education in the Travelling Community. Spurned by ordinary society (many schools refused to accept their children) Sr Colette decided to start a special school for them in Bray. She negotiated and bought the Christian Brothers' old school at Walcot, Old Connaught Avenue, with the support of people like Sheila Pim, Victor Bewley, and the Archbishop of Dublin, the late Dr McQuaid.

Unfortunately, some time after this the premises at Walcot were destroyed by fire, but, undeterred, Sr Colette managed to procure prefabs, with the help of John Tansey and other friends, and kept the school going.

She had been involved in setting up the Training Centre in Ennis for the young Travellers there and she saw the real need there was for a similar one in the South Co. Dublin/North Wicklow area — and so the old premises at Walcot became St Kieran's Training Centre.

Like the school at that time, the Training Centre had no public funding so the task was formidable — no one else could have had the courage and determination to overcome such obstacles. She was lucky that she found a person of like mind to herself in the first director of the Training Centre, Michael Bermingham. Both she and Michael firmly believed in going to the top people and never taking 'no' for an answer, and so Co. Dublin VEC was persuaded to pay the teachers and AnCO (now FÁS) agreed to pay a training allowance to the young Travelling boys and girls who enrolled there. People like Jerry Cronin and the VEC; with Pat O'Shea and John Horgan of AnCO took a personal interest in the centre, and St Kieran's would not have survived without them.

St Kieran's, too, was lucky to have a dedicated group of teachers in those early days. People like Mena Darcy, Sean

Doyle, Tom Finn, John Byrne, Joan Merrigan, all worked miracles with the very limited materials available. Under their guidance the young trainees produced beautiful patchwork quilts, children's clothes, wrought iron and wood craftwork, which were sold, and so helped to raise money to keep the Centre going. With grants now available from both the VEC and FÁS what a difference there is, and the curriculum now includes literacy, life skills and sports, as well as the craftwork.

Living conditions for the Travellers in those days were even more horrendous than they are now. Many families lived in tarpaulin tents in water-logged ditches and fields, and so to campaign for better conditions Sr Colette set up a special committee which constantly protested about the situation. South Co. Dublin and Dun Laoghaire Councils did set up some special housing and sites in their areas (though not nearly enough), but Wicklow did nothing in this regard until very recently, despite intense pressure on the authorities there over the years.

This is only a short resume of Sr Colette's work in the Bray area. Her whole life has been devoted to the cause of the Travelling People all over the country, and it is important that recognition should be given to her pioneering work in this often unpopular sphere. I salute a remarkable woman, whom it is a privilege to know.

Kathleen Kinsella

When I was first introduced to Sr Colette Dwyer at a Fashion Show in 1979, the clothes for which were made and modelled by the students of St Kieran's Training Centre, I little thought that I would become involved with Travellers and with St Kieran's School in particular, and that this involvement would continue to the present day. Sr Colette was, and still is, very persuasive in recruiting people to help her with her work with the Travelling Community.

I started work in St Kieran's in March of 1979. The school was housed in a prefabricated building which had seen better days. It consisted of four classrooms, a kitchen, a bathroom and a clothes store, which became known as 'the boutique'. There was also an office and a staffroom.

Mairin Kenny was Principal. Also on the staff were Sheila Keatings, Maureen Dowling and Noreen Feely. Sheila had been on the staff at St Kieran's since its beginning. Mrs Peggy Grogan, a nurse who came to help at the school during Lent one year and who stayed for ten years — another of Sr Colette's 'volunteers' — looked after the health and hygiene of the children.

There were very few families in permanent accommodation then and there were no official sites. There was a very large encampment in Killiney, called Hacketsland and another in Bray. This was in a field, owned by a gentleman called Billy Cassells. Children also came from Ballyogan, Cabinteely, Leopardstown, Foxrock, Sallynoggin and from different parts of Bray and North Wicklow.

We had one minibus. Mick Rafferty, the driver, gave unstintingly of his time, often having to do three runs each morning, lunch time and afternoon to get the children to and from school.

Because school was a new experience for our pupils some found it difficult to stay in the classroom for any length of time. Very often the doors had to be locked and even then the more intrepid climbed out of the windows. Also, family groups liked to be together, the oldest member was always responsible for his/her siblings. Mairin Kenny had a great understanding of Traveller culture and allowed members of the same family to stay together until they got used to the school and trusted the teachers.

Sr Colette was a very frequent visitor. She was most supportive of the staff and extremely generous with funding. She was aware of the importance of broadening the experience of the children and managed to provide for outings, Christmas parties and annual residential holidays. These were thoroughly enjoyed by all, though exhausting for the teachers who gave so generously of their time.

As I got to know and love the Travelling children I learned to appreciate their disingenuous openness and their lack of pretence. Many of them were related. It was quite common to have an aunt or uncle who was younger than his or her niece or nephew. And since there were so many relatives there were few surnames; the most common were Connors, Moorhouse and O'Brien. To distinguish children with the the same christian and surname, pet names were used. These were lovely — we had a Miss Moo, Boyo, Mud Womans, Mickey Mouse, Girl, Johnny Jinks, Bangalang and others. As the children grew older they allowed only family, friends and people they trusted to call them by these names.

Over the years Sr Colette was busy putting her case for a new building to each successive Minister for Education. In 1982 persistence was rewarded and a new school was sanctioned by the Department, though a few years were to lapse before this materialised.

In the meantime the prefab deteriorated; the roof leaked, the floors gave way, the windows rotted and we were infested with rats. Despite valiant and expensive efforts on the part of Sr Colette and her Board of Management to keep the structure together we were forced to abandon ship in 1986.

We were indeed fortunate to find generous benefactors in the Community of Christian Brothers in Mount St Mary, close to Old Connaught Avenue. The Brothers went out of their way to make us welcome and we spent a happy and valuable four years in exile. We had told the Brothers that we would need refuge for only one year, but we were never made to feel that we had out stayed our welcome.

During this period our numbers increased and we hired a second minibus. The children loved coming to school, and with the provision of three group housing schemes and one authorised halting site attendance was more regular. As a result, the standard of achievement improved in leaps and bounds.

In 1990 we moved back to our old site, but instead of a run-down prefab we had a magnificent new building with landscaped gardens and a well laid out playground. What a joy it was, and still is, to work in such a comfortable and well-planned school. The homely atmosphere it generates is something we value. The children and staff are justly proud of their school. Sr Colette's persistence has paid handsome dividends: we now have six classrooms, a beautiful assembly area, a PE hall and a pre-school as well as a kitchen, laundry and bathroom. It is a fitting tribute to Sr Colette's dedication to the education of the children of the Travelling Community.

Throughout my years at St Kieran's I have seen a tremendous improvement in the attitude of Travelling parents to education. Many of the children attending St Kieran's are the sons and daughters of former pupils. Also the housing and halting site situation has improved though there is still a long way to go before all our families are adequately accommodated. The hard work and dedication of Sr Colette and Mairin Kenny and her staff have been well rewarded. Three minibuses and a fifty-two seater coach are now needed to carry the children to and from school. And following a general inspection by the Department of

Education earlier this year it was found that many of the pupils are well up to the expected standard for their age.

In sixteen years I have come to know Sr Colette well. Her energy and drive never ceases to amaze me, as does her ability to chair three or four meetings in a day, and to have facts and figures for each at her fingertips. I admire her courage and her vision and her ability to get things done: I don't think she understands the meaning of the word 'no'! Her understanding and love of the Travelling Community, and the provision she made for the education of their children at a time when nothing was being done impressed me greatly. Sr Colette should feel justly proud of her achievements and I feel honoured to be counted among her many friends.

Rose Lamb

I FIRST heard the name Sr Colette Dwyer as I moved about on the roads as a Traveller, whenever the subject of our rights, or the lack of them came up.

You heard people say that she was a great nun, and if you had any problems you could always contact her, and you'd be sure that she would always do her best for you.

When I became involved with people representing Travellers, and trying to have some of the changes made where necessary, it quickly became clear to me just how much she had achieved for us all, and the painstaking efforts she had made throughout the country, receiving abuse from time to time, and little acknowledgement for all the long hours travelling to and from meetings etc., always trying to get us to represent ourselves more and more, while reminding us of our dignity and self-respect, and our equal rights.

There came a time when I needed some advice on things

that were bothering me, so I decided to contact this great lady. When I finally got to speak to her on the phone, I suggested that I would go to Galway to see her, but she wouldn't hear of this, and instead came to see me — again reflecting her willingness to shoulder the yoke.

When she arrived at my house in Mayo, I was surprised that she looked so much younger than her years, and her fluency of thought and speech far exceeded the average person, and I knew very quickly that here was a woman from whom I could learn a great deal.

She commended me on the level of education I had received, and encouraged me to believe that it would be a great plus to go on and take my Leaving Certificate, so that I could help the Traveller community to go as far as they could in education throughout the country. I am now doing just that.

I have since had a number of meetings with Sr Colette and some of her friends who are involved with the cause of the Travelling people, and I have learn much from her and them, though she always says that we all learned from one another. There are many people to thank for their efforts in helping the Travelling people, but none more so than Sr Colette Dwyer. We were blessed that she came among us, and as long as she remains involved we can only continue to improve.

Gus Sweeney

As I have endeavoured to collect matter for this book, and asked for contributions from people who worked with Colette from the earliest days of her involvement with the Travellers, I feel it incumbent to add my own tale of how I myself became involved.

"Would You Ever Teach Us to Read, Sister?"

I would first of all like to say here that my 24 years in Ireland have undoubtedly been the happiest of my whole life, 22 of those years I have actually spent living with Colette, and I very quickly became interested in her work, and through it made many friends, both Travellers and settled people.

Colette had been my Headmistress when I taught in England, and later my Superior (or Reverend Mother as it was called in those days). To be quite frank, when it was suggested that we would live together as a community of two, and I would be of what help I could to promote the work, I did not think the experiment would last very long. I am a very ordinary sort of person, and my idea of Colette was that she was highly intellectual. So I had visions of our conversations petering out quite quickly, and finding common grounds of interest and contact becoming more and more difficult. How wrong I was! Not only did our common interest in the Travellers bind us together, as well as our home-making and the work in Lough Graney, but I found we shared many interests, e.g. taste in music, in books, in praying together etc. and Colette did not talk highfalutin philosophy, which I wouldn't even understand.

So, from my point of view things worked out very happily, and the more I travelled around with her all over the country to Travellers' encampments, classes, schools and Training Centres, the more I realised that her whole life was lived for the betterment of Travellers.

There was absolutely no avenue she would not go down if she thought there was even a faint possibility of achieving a solution to one of their problems.

She always went to the very top — Minister, not just their officials — with her requests (demands?). I did hear that in one Government Department, officials used to 'run for cover' if they saw her approach, and had not fulfilled her last request!

She herself was a perfectionist in everything she did, and was intolerant of anyone who promised to do something, and was then dilatory in carrying out whatever they had promised her they would do! In fact, she always held that she was not a practical person, but when the need arose we found that this was indeed an erroneous assumption. In my own invalid years, I could not have wished for a more caring and capable person.

Where she had expected promises to be fulfilled even before she had asked for them, so in practical matters she noticed what was needed, and provided it almost before it had been asked for.

I can only end this by saying that my estimation of Colette was, and still is, that she is an amazingly dedicated women.

Sr Cyprian Unsworth

ALTHOUGH I knew Sr Colette slightly from about 1967 onwards, it wasn't until 1972 that I got to know her well, but even in 1967 our paths were beginning to run in parallel lines. We were both touched by the plight of the Travelling People at about the same time. We had both been influenced by what we had read and heard about them from Victor Bewley and Father Tom Fehily, and their efforts on behalf of the Travellers.

While Sr Colette was starting to work on the lack of educational facilities available to them, I was starting on the long haul to persuade Local Authorities to provide decent accommodation for them. Little did we know what lay ahead, in the attitudes of sections of the settled community towards our work.

I know that Sr Colette received more than her fair share of abuse, intimidation and misunderstanding. The risk of personal danger was never far away in those early days and we learned to live with it.

Sr Colette always had amazing courage and tenacity, and, with a small committee of like-minded people, she obtained a 5-acre site in south Co. Dublin, where a school, St Kieran's, for Traveller children was opened within the year, followed by five chalets for families to live in, and later on a Training Centre. This was a milestone in many ways, firstly because it proved decisively that Travelling children who had never had an opportunity to attend school could and would come, that they were as bright as any group of settled children, and what was more, they enjoyed learning.

A segregated school for Traveller children did not become the norm, and when, some years later, the Department of Education became actively involved in the financing of education for Travellers, it opted for integration into the National School system. It did, however, eventually see the need for Special Classes within the schools for those who had missed out on early education, or were for whatever reason unable to keep up with the class.

As the work gathered momentum, Sr Colette found (in her own words) that 'visiting schools, social workers, Inspectors etc., and identifying facilities of any kind' was absolutely full-time, and in September of 1972 things began to change. First of all, she and I were sent by the National Council as part of a delegation invited by the Dutch Government to visit Holland. Fr Christy Jones (now Bishop of Elphin) from Sligo, was the third delegate. The trip was sponsored by the Dutch Government Ministry of Culture and Recreation and the purpose of it was 'to study the work done by the Government to solve the problem of the 35,000 Travelling People in

Holland. It was a wonderful experience — a week of being driven around from one beautiful campsite to the next, meeting teachers, officials and social workers, with opportunities to talk, through an interpreter unfortunately, to the Travellers in their elegant mobile homes (from which the wheels had all been removed) and to their children in their splendidly equipped schools. We learned a lot about what can be done by a well-meaning government, with almost unlimited resources, to solve their problems, but also with no prior consultation with the Travellers themselves, thus creating even bigger problems for the future.

We also learned a lot about each other. We were an unusual trio — a nun, a priest and a Protestant widow! Every evening we talked, learned, argued and laughed! We became friends. It was shortly after that period that Sr Colette and I changed our status from being voluntary workers to full-time employees of the National Council. We officially became National Co-ordinators for Education and Accommodation respectively. This involved a considerable amount of travelling for both of us, together with frequent contact with officialdom. Reports and surveys, meetings and speaking at meetings filled our days. But always our main concern was to maintain our contact with Travellers themselves, and with the local Voluntary Committees throughout the country. The workload for Sr Colette was awesome, and one wonders how her health has stood up to it. No sooner had she set up one project to meet a particular need, than she was off again on another. Her list of achievements is mind-boggling. In her own words: 'the main objectives of the work were to identify the educational needs of the Travelling People, and to ensure that as many Traveller children as possible could avail of educational and training opportunities, according to their own needs and aspirations'. This she did, and it is my belief that no one else could have done it.

Joyce Sholdice

IT WAS almost ten years ago that I first met Sr Colette Dwyer. Emerging from full-time motherhood, I was looking for an opportunity to put my social science training to good use. The situation of the Travelling People was something which had troubled me for a long, long time. I called in unexpectedly one day to speak to Mr Victor Bewley whose name I associated with the Travellers, looking for direction. It was he who suggested that I contact St Kieran's Training Centre and St Kieran's National School in Bray, Co. Wicklow. He assured me that my offer of help would be welcomed there! And so it was that I was invited to become a member of the South Co. Dublin Committee for the Settlement of Travellers, and first met Sr Colette, who was chairperson of this committee. Her fame went before her, and I quickly learned of her considerable achievements in the field of education for young Travellers. At a time when the Traveller cause was not a popular one, she set up a network of 27 Training Centres throughout the country, specially focussed on the educational and training needs of teenagers, male and female. She succeeded in persuading FÁS (AnCO as it was then) and the VEC to fund these centres, no mean feat! These centres are flourishing today, and being involved both as a teacher and a member of the Board of Management, I can say from personal experience, the marvellous resource they are for young Travellers.

Travellers' rights is another area in which Sr Colette has immersed herself wholeheartedly. Again, at the time when

Traveller issues were very low down on the political agenda, Sr Colette managed to attract the attention of the senior politicians of the day and persuaded them to focus their departments' attention on matters such as Travellers accommodation. As a result of her endeavours, a monitoring body has been set up to oversee developments in these areas.

These are only two of the many areas relating to Travellers, in which I have been involved alongside Sr Colette, I know she is active in many, many more.

At a time when lesser mortals are enjoying an easier lifestyle after a life-time of very hard work, Sr Colette only seems to be getting her second wind! Her energy seems boundless. She still has that marvellous charisma which draws people towards her and she still has the capacity to attract men and women of considerable influence and power, to champion her causes.

Her gentle manner and soft speech belie a steely determination when it comes to issues of Travellers' rights. I have seen grown men and women quiver in their shoes, if they have failed to deliver on a promise to her!

It is this stubbornness and implacability which have ensured that her campaign on behalf of Travellers has known the success it has.

Long may she continue!

Gari McKeown

13

TRAVELLERS' VIEWS ON THEIR EDUCATIONAL EXPERIENCE

RECENTLY a simple questionnaire was sent out to Literacy Teachers in a number of Training Centres. The teachers were asked to elicit as many responses as possible from their ex-trainees. The findings discussed below represent a 'synthesis' of responses from six counties that replied. The most informative aspect of the exercise was the striking similarity between answers.

The majority of the Travellers who answered the questionnaire had spent an average of eight years attending primary school. Few had attended a pre-school, though several started primary school at five. Many did not begin until they were seven and nearly all said they attended regularly.

Most said they were able to read and write at the end of their schooling, though some said 'only a little'.

Most said they did not enjoy school at all for reasons such as they did not like 'sitting down all day'. Nearly all said they 'didn't mind the teachers'.

Most said that they enjoyed their Training Centres because they 'learned how to do lots of things' or that they 'got to know that they could do things they thought they couldn't do'. Nearly all said that they would take their children away when they were twelve or thirteen. There was general agreement that special help should be provided for children who started school late, or were not able to attend regularly.

Those who had attended a pre-school unanimously agreed that they were helpful. There was also general agreement that Travelling children should be treated 'the same as other children' and that they would like their children to go to a school for 'country people'.

A number said they attended school for two thirds of most years, as they travelled from April to September, and some stressed that parents should be strongly encouraged to send them to school every day and said 'the system should be more strict on the parents. I would love to go back to school but my father won't let me'. Nearly all said that they wanted the very best education for their children.

The remainder of this chapter is devoted to the reflections of two Travellers who have availed of educational opportunities.

THE importance of early education for the overall development of the pre-school child has long been established and recognised by educationalists, psychologists, social workers and parents. Therefore it must go without saying just how vital the pre-school services are for the Traveller child.

The reason I say this is that we only have to look at the high illiteracy rate amongst adult Travellers and the low attendance levels of Travelling children attending primary school to understand the necessity for this important service (pre-school).

Formal education i.e. primary schools with the negative attitudes held by the Traveller parent have contributed towards the situation we are now faced with in education in general — early school leavers, erratic attenders, high unemployment and virtually no integration.

I have been teaching for five years in a pre-school designated for Travelling children. I have seen many positive results in the overall development of the Traveller child and the slow input of the parents involvement in the recognition of the credibility of pre-school education. In my use of the word 'slow' I think its important that people outside the Travelling Community, especially educationalists, recognise the changing attitudes of the young Traveller parent. Initially, many parents were dubious of the overall benefits of the pre-school, I think its also important to point out that I, not only as a teacher but also as a Traveller, have been able to convince parents of the need for children's regular attendance at school. Pre-school has been looked upon as a child-minding service rather than a haven of knowledge. Needless to say this convincing took a lot of time but it has eventually paid off. Parents have begun to realise and recognise their child as an individual with massive potential and ability to absorb basic skills i.e. fine motor skills, language, numbers, letters and most importantly the building of inner discipline leading to overall concentration of mind and body.

Many children come from large families and lack individual attention and perhaps at times social courtesy. If the child learns nothing else in the pre-school he/she at least learns how to interact socially with their own age group and adults.

I am glad to say that over the past five years I have seen past pupils attend regularly as we have good working relationships with the schools. I have found that the majority of our past pupils are integrating fully in the school environment.

Personally I believe that the fact that I was fortunate to

avail of education up to third level has shaped my ideas and made me adamant about the future of Travellers in the educational system. I think it is very important that Travellers should be involved as teachers and child-care assistants, this I would see as a very positive approach in the changing of many of the negative feelings Travellers' parents have about education.

We (the Travelling Community) need more role models to encourage our young people to further advance their education.

In conclusion, children come into this world without prejudice or any preconceived notion about others, I believe it is time we recognised how imperative it is to break down the barriers between the different cultures in Irish society.

I hope one day to see mixed pre-schools rather than all Traveller ones, where all children can learn and love each other.

Ellen Mongan

THE demands on Travelling children and the problems they face in school requires special knowledge and a deep understanding of their background.

While talking to a number of teachers who are involved in teaching Traveller children they agreed that a better understanding of Traveller culture would be of great benefit to them.

I think that a module about Traveller culture and lifestyle should be introduced into teacher training courses, it would give the teacher an appreciation and a greater understanding of the positive and valued areas of the Traveller way of life.

I was fortunate enough to avail of education from primary

to third level. However I would like to add that without the support of my parents and family this would not have been possible. My parents took a keen interest in my education, unfortunately not all Traveller parents do likewise. However, this attitude is changing slowly especially among younger parents.

While the children of Travellers receive adequate love and affection from their families many receive little in the way of stimulation during infancy and early childhood. Their parents usually have little understanding of the importance of early play, and reading and talking to young children on an individual basis. Consequently, by the time the majority of Traveller children reach school age they are already delayed in many areas of development and learning, many also have speech problems. Therefore, many are disadvantaged, from an educational point of view, from birth. This is why the pre-school is of vital importance to the early development of the Traveller child.

Being able to avail of third level education opened up many doors for me. Not only was I able to meet with different people, with varied outlooks, it also helped me develop a greater understanding of other minority groups. I also had the opportunity to make very good friends with settled people who had little or no contact with Travellers up until then. As friendships formed many of their fears about Travellers disintegrated. I count myself very fortunate to have been able to experience an education that will benefit me for the rest of my life.

In future considerations of Traveller education a clear plan should be established which would bring about a gradual move away from all forms of segregated education. In order to bring about changes successfully, the Department of Education would have to consider the special needs of mainstream education. Plans should be made for the provision of adequate remedial teaching and sufficient visiting teachers to help the children attain the required academic standards.

In the long-term education offers us (Travellers) the best hope of improving our situation. It is only through education that we will gain a better understanding of our rights and needs, as well as our responsibilities.

Without education many of the serious social and health problems which beset Travellers at the present time cannot be alleviated and the children will not be able to enjoy the quality of life enjoyed by most other children in Ireland today.

Education must be a priority for all Traveller children in Ireland.

Caroline Ward

14

DREAMS AND HOPES FOR THE FUTURE

I suppose my greatest dream is that as the new century approaches Travellers will be recognised and accepted for what they are and will contribute to Irish Society, to which we all belong. Specifically I hope we will see an end to discrimination, ostracisation, and the blaming of the whole Traveller Community for the wrong-doings of a few.

A very large percentage of the settled community ('country people' as the Travellers call them) has consistently tarred them all with the same brush, and attributed to all the obvious failure of a small number. As the Travellers themselves often say, 'there is often a rotten apple in every basket', and they do not maintain that they are any different in this regard. The main trouble is, as mentioned earlier in this book, few members of the settled community have ever even spoken to a Traveller, let alone made any effort to get to know them as the lovely people I have found them to be.

Although little has been said in this book on the subject of accommodation, since its subject is primarily education/training and employment, the provision of adequate accommodation for Traveller families, is inextricably interwoven with educational provision and development. It is a *sine qua non* that if you have no settled place in which to live, you cannot possibly avail of the educational opportunities to which every child and adult in the country has a constitutional right. The Government has promised that it intends to have such accommodation available to all Travellers by the year 2000. My hope is that no family will be forced to live in accommodation about which they have not been consulted, or in a place which is abhorrent to them for one reason or another.

In the field of education, one of my dreams is that every Traveller child will eventually have the opportunity to attend a pre-school, where basic skills can be absorbed. One of the main problems teachers receiving Traveller children into primary school encounter is the limited nature of the child's vocabulary. This is not surprising when one considers that there are few (if any) books in a Traveller home, and that the majority of the adult population of Travellers is illiterate. In the pre-school, as Ellen Mongan has ably described in the previous chapter, the children can be taught all kinds of language and other relevant skills which will prepare them for entrance into mainstream education. Only a tiny percentage of Traveller children at present attend one of the 53 pre-schools in the country.

Another dream would be that all Traveller children entering mainstream education at primary level would be welcomed and made to feel at home. There are still far too many examples of Travellers being ridiculed, called derogatory names, and even shunned by their fellow pupils in some schools. These incidences have done nothing to encourage them to feel accepted by the settled community, can cause the development in later years of a positive sense of being 'a race apart', and result in antagonistic, and sometimes, anti-social behaviour. This can lead to serious trouble in adult life.

Dreams and Hopes

I have long campaigned for courses to be made available in all teacher training colleges to help future teachers to understand Traveller children, their culture, traditions, and background, so that a better understanding between them and their Traveller pupils may be established more quickly. Teachers could then also prepare their settled pupils for the acceptance of Travellers in their midst.

One of my most cherished dreams, and one which I did not succeed in fulfilling myself, has always been to see the majority of Traveller children proceeding to post-primary education. I told the Visiting Teachers when I ceased to be National Co-ordinator, that had I felt able to continue in the work, I would have made this area my priority. I know they have since continued to work on this. For reasons which I have gone into more fully in this book, however, there are many obstacles in the way of achieving my dream. The attitude of the majority of parents, along with the firmly held view within the Traveller Community, that Confirmation equals graduation, and that all children of 12+ should be working in the home, or to augment the family income, means that if the children continue at school after the age of 12, they will not have the support of their parents, and in many cases will be positively discouraged from so doing. It is not easy for a Traveller child to make a lonely decision to continue his/her education when there is no incentive from home to do so.

The recent White Paper does not seem to produce many ideas on how to persuade children of 12+ and their parents to go down this road. It will be interesting to see how much commitment the new 'Education Board' will have, as well as how much imagination and knowledge of these families it will show. Persuasion, and the imaginative programmes in the better Junior Training Centres, as well as the careful choice of committed teachers and Directors, have proved the only successes to date, and the VEC must be commended for this. We have tried post-primary and VEC ordinary schools, but only occasionally have they been successful in keeping their Travellers for very long. I place my trust in the Visiting Teachers, whom I know have the interests of these children at heart, as well as the commitment to achieve success.

The appreciation expressed in previous White Papers of Junior Training Centres, allied with a policy of closing them down, will not bring a single extra pupil in secondary education.

My dreams for the future for the Travellers extend way beyond secondary school education. Now that about a dozen of them, mainly in Galway and Cork, have achieved third level education and qualified to work as teachers and community workers for their own people, I think a breakthrough has been made. This year's election of the first Traveller woman to be a town councillor by the votes of the settled and Traveller communities, was a great breakthrough for the Travellers, and when later she was nominated and chosen (one of seven out of 700 nominations) to be a 1994 Person of the Year, and was asked by Dick Spring where she hoped to go from there, I was delighted to hear her reply, 'To the Dáil, of course'.

There is no end to how far Travellers could go if only they were given the chance. In her article in the previous chapter, Ellen Mongan does not say that it took her five years to become a Montessori teacher, with an English qualification, which she had to obtain by correspondence course.

There has to be a lot of cooperation from parents if a son or daughter wants to go on to third level education. Here in Galway a wonderful mother made it possible for two of her daughters to do just that, even though her husband died half way through their course, and she has a very large family and poor health.

One of her daughters (Caroline Ward) has written in this book.

Travellers are now so articulate and so well able to speak for themselves, that, thank God, they no longer need settled people to do it for them. They would be well able to represent their community in the Dáil, and it would be wonderful to see them there.

My final dream is the establishment of other Employment Centres such as St Kieran's Enterprise Centre in Dublin. We do have another in Tuam, but it still has a long way to go before achieving its full potential.

Finally, I must say something about Adult Education which is my main work today. When I left the adult classes which had been my first encounter with Travellers, I told the adults that I felt I must go and do something for their children, none of whom were at the time attending school regularly, but that I would return to them before my work ended.

So now, in my end is my beginning, and the adults are now my most important concern. It is all the more important, because, as their children avail more and more of education at all levels, the parents feel more and more inadequate.

The Department of Education has made it possible for me to set up groups in various parts of the country, which local people are willing to staff, for adults who are keen to learn basic literacy, and other skills. I think they are doing marvellous work, and when their annual reports come in I am more and more impressed by the variety of the needs which they are meeting. Unfortunately, the men are much less inclined to take part in these activities than the women, but gradually, in some areas men are beginning to ask for courses more suitable to them. It is a pleasure to visit these groups and see what progress they are making, and how much they enjoy the activities on offer.

"Would You Ever Teach Us to Read, Sister?"

I suppose I will never stop dreaming until I am dead, so perhaps I should stop this dream right here with a big 'thank you' to all the men, women and children of the Traveller Community who have given me so much during the last 28 years, and to those who have worked so devotedly for them.